Scream Writing:

A Comprehensive Guide to Writing

the Horror Screenplay

By

Zack Long

Printed in the United States of America

First Printing, October 2019
Second Edition

ISBN-13: 978-1-7336817-7-3

Table of Contents

Introduction

I was far too young the first time I saw *The Evil Dead* (1981).

When I was in grade school, I spent a long weekend at a family friend's house. I was allowed to stay up late, and, best of all, I was able to play ignorant about not being allowed to watch *Army of Darkness* (1992). Medieval skeletons, demon-zombie-monster-things (Deadites, I know now), and a badass hero with a chainsaw for a hand and a shotgun strapped to his back. It was my every childhood fantasy come to life and it was groovy.

When I got back home I admitted what I had seen and I talked about how awesome it was and how there really wasn't anything that bad in it (and there wasn't). So … can I watch the first one? Please Mom and Dad?

If you haven't seen it, *The Evil Dead* really is something. A rollercoaster of unrelenting terror, blood and guts splattered against every surface. There's no groovy action hero. There's just a handful of kids that have got themselves trapped in hell with no way out and whoever made this film must have been a madman. An absolute maniac, real in touch with the devil.

There wasn't even a chainsaw hand.

The Evil Dead changed my life. I had always been into the scary side of film and media, always dressed up as monsters, and Halloween was my favorite season. But *The*

Evil Dead scared me in a way nothing had ever scared me before. It drove an obsession.

I watched the film hundreds of times on VHS. When I got my hands on the DVDs, I listened to the commentary tracks so many times that I had memorized them word for word. I had to devour it all, to figure out how it was done so I could drain it of its horrible power.

One fact led to another. I learned a technique used for the camera work and that led me to researching other material in order to understand why it was different and what it meant. Geocities site after Geocities site.

Somewhere along the way I truly fell in love with the genre.

My obsession with the horror genre fuelled my decision in leaving my creative writing studies at Dalhousie University in my third year due to the animosity that it was receiving within academia. I have been writing horror for nearly two decades now, and have been reading the academic literature on the horror film that has flourished within those same decades. There was a respectability to the genre that only a handful seemed to understand—primarily within film studies but there was also a comradery between horror fans that is predicated specifically on the outsider status this understanding gives them.

The horror genre is misunderstood.

It's Frankenstein's Monster.

———————————————

Kelly Warner, author of the post-apocalypse kaiju trilogy *In the Shadow of Extinction,* wrote about how she feels the advice "write what you know" often gets misinterpreted. I believe a similar piece of writing advice has also gotten misinterpreted. Except rather than the people receiving the advice, I feel it is the people giving it that are mistaken. What piece of advice is that you ask? It's that age old horror hand me down:

"Write What Scares You"

So here's the thing: if you're scared of spiders and you write *Eight Legged Freaks 2*, that's fantastic if what you wanted to do was to write *Eight Legged Freaks 2*. If someone suggested listing your fears out and using what scares you to scare the audience and you came up with spiders so you wrote it because that's how you thought you would become a horror writer, then that's not so fantastic. The problem with writing what scares us is that a lot of us aren't able to get into those deep dark places of our psyche where our fears really lie.

And, frankly, what if you don't give a single shit for writing about spiders? I know that I don't, and I'm absolutely terrified of them.

When it comes to writing scary stories, be they film or prose, it is my belief that the deeper fears we hold will find a way to manifest themselves through our characters and our tone. The horror genre is such a primal place that a lot of unconscious themes rise within our stories. The genre often allows for a Freudian release; is it any wonder that the horror film and psychoanalysis have been so closely tied within academia?

The genre has also been used for so much more. Simon Barrett, writer of *You're Next* (2011) and *The Guest* (2014), mentioned on an episode of Red Letter Media's *Re:View* that the impetus to write *You're Next* came not from a fear of home invasion but from a complaint he heard about how many home invasion movies were just people tied to chairs.

The late Wes Craven, writer and director of *A Nightmare on Elm Street* (1984), spoke often about the inspiration for the legendary slasher film. The idea of a boogeyman that gets you in your sleep came from a newspaper article he read about a young man who thought that if he went to sleep, he would die; sure enough, when he next went to sleep he never woke. However, the idea for Freddy Krueger came from recalling a man that did scare Craven when he was younger. However, that memory wasn't where he went looking for the idea—he found an idea and that memory was able to help later on.

This piece of advice keeps coming up in so many of the "How To Write Horror" books that are on the market. These books would have you believe that it's the "show, don't tell" of the horror genre. But the truth is that, frankly, it's hard to be scared of our own writing. And that's fine, our goal isn't to scare ourselves.

It's to scare them.

The journey of Scream Writing was a circuitous path. My first attempts at structuring and exploring the topic all seemed too loose. Indeed, that's one of my problems when it comes to reading books on writing. The first volume I ever bought on writing horror screenplays spent pages telling me the various tools I could use: pen, paper, programs. Of course, half of those programs are gone now and I already knew that you could write with a pen. It was Screenwriting 101 but I was looking to dive into horror. In looking to avoid the same trap I was able to find the book's structure.

Each chapter focuses on one of the major elements of the horror film: its history, monsters, scares, settings, and plots. In this way the focus is kept strongly on the horror side. In this I expect the reader to know how to write a script—that is, the physical blocking of the page—or has access to the plethora of free materials available online that lay it out for them. I make the expectation that the reader is someone who is already writing and looking to expand their knowledge base rather than a complete novice.

My approach to teaching is to explore the theories and reasoning behind our creative decisions. I believe that understanding how the tools we use create a cognitive effect within the audience is the key to writing the most effective and impactful stories. Each chapter ends with some exercises (or, in the case of Chapter 1, materials for further study) to help the Scream Writer digest the material and put it into action in their screamplays.

The writing process is filled with discoveries that I hope further your relationship with writing horror. Most important of all, don't forget to have fun. In horror we explore dark territories; and as writers, we are often prone to getting lost within the worlds we create or forgetting the simple fact: this is supposed to be fun. Parts of the creative journey are exhilarating but parts of it are frustrating as hell. Try to remember it is a balance, neither side lasts forever. Enjoy the good, push through the bad, and scare the hell out of the audience.

Chapter 1: The Genre

The history of horror movies goes back a long way ... of people trying to convincingly be terrified when looking at a piece of tape on the side of the camera box. I have a whole new respect for it.

Josh Hamilton

It's my belief that an understanding of horror film history will help Scream Writers to craft their most effective and compelling scripts. In the words of George Santayana, "those who cannot remember the past are condemned to repeat it." But, as the success of Quentin Tarantino shows, the quote could be appended for Scream Writers to read "those who cannot remember the past are unable to reinvent it."

This chapter will explore the challenge of defining the horror genre, chart its history from the dawn of cinema through to what the future holds, and briefly touch on why we won't be focusing on specific subgenres (as well as provide resources for those that wish to stick their hands deep in the subgenre grime). We will then finish, as every chapter will, with some exercises to put what we've learned into action and improve our Scream Writing skills.

Definition of Horror

Before we embark on the actual writing of the horror screenplay, we must first understand what it is we mean when we refer to the horror genre. The *Oxford English Dictionary* defines 'horror' as "an intense feeling of fear, shock, or disgust." Further, it specifies that as a modifier 'horror' is "a literary or film genre concerned with arousing feelings of horror." Alright, so a horror film would be a film that endeavoured to provoke fear, shock, or disgust within the viewer.

If this definition seems too easy, that's because it is. While *Oxford*'s definition is a testament to brevity, it only serves to raise further questions: If the genre is concerned with arousing feelings of horror, does that mean that *Winnie the Pooh* is a horror film for someone with arkoudaphobia (the fear of bears)? Where is the line between horror and thriller? Could a film about pregnancy, say *Juno* (2007) or *Junior* (1994), be considered a horror film if it provoked fear, shock, or disgust when watched by someone who doesn't want kids.

In attempting to understand the paradoxical nature of the horror genre—that someone would not just willingly but gladly subject themselves to the emotional experience of a horror film —Noel Carroll penned the aptly named *The Philosophy of Horror, or Paradoxes of the Heart*. Carroll spends nearly three-hundred pages exploring what he calls "**art-horror.**" For Carroll, a separation between horror and "art-horror" explains our desire to watch these films (or read these novels, stories, etc). To be "art-horrified" not only requires that the audiences' emotions are a reflection of the protagonists but that:

1) [They are] in some state of abnormal, physically felt agitation (shuddering, tingling, screaming, etc.) which 2) has been *caused* by a) the thought: that Dracula is a possible being; and by the evaluative thoughts: that b) said Dracula has the property of being physically (and perhaps morally and socially) threatening in the ways portrayed in fiction and that c) said Dracula has the property of being impure, where 3) such thoughts are usually accompanied by the desire to avoid the touch of things like Dracula. (27)

While this idea of being "art-horrified" has been an invaluable resource for those approaching the horror film from an affect studies framework, it doesn't serve to simplify or clarify our understanding of the genre anymore than the *Oxford English Dictionary* has. Carroll sees being "art-horrified" as the primary goal of the horror genre. Barry Keith Grant agrees with Carroll when he writes in *Screams on Screens: Paradigms of Horror* that horror is primarily concerned with its effect rather than its content.

Writer Douglas Winter would agree, as he wrote in his 1982 anthology *Prime Evil*, that "Horror is not a genre, like the mystery or science fiction or the western. It is not a kind of fiction, meant to be confined to the ghetto of a special shelf in libraries or bookstores. Horror is an emotion." If horror is not a genre then how is it that video stores, Netflix, or the libraries that Winter mentioned have been able to sort and categorize these films under the heading of horror? If a horror film fails to scare the viewer is it still a horror film?

George Ochoa offers a different perspective, one that specifically orients itself against Carroll's. Ochoa wrote in *Deformed and Destructive Beings: The Purpose of Horror Films* that Carroll was misidentifying "the locus of audience gratification from horror" which Carroll said wasn't the monster in the story but was instead "the whole narrative structure in which the presentation of the monster is staged" (1). Ochoa uses his book to put forth what he described as "a materialist-teleological-hetero-ontologic-Rortian-pragmatist-Aristotelian-Thomist theory of horror films" (16). This is a lot of words—too many—to explain that Ochoa's theory places the displaying of the monster as the entire purpose of the horror film.

It is these *Deformed and Destructive Beings* that draw us towards the horrific, be they deformed and destructive in a physical sense such as in *The Blob* (1958), *The Evil Dead* and *Basketcase* (1982), or deformed and destructive in a psychological sense such as Norman Bates in *Psycho* (1960), Leatherface in *The Texas Chainsaw Massacre* (1974), or the vast majority of slasher movie villains: Jason Voorhees, Michael Myers, Angela Baker, Harry Warden, Jack Torrance, Billy, or Ghostface. But what about those films that seem to lack a character definable as deformed and destructive?

One might claim there is a witch in *The Blair Witch Project* (1999), but the true horror of the film is the experience of being lost in the woods. And while some may consider it too sci-fi to be included within horror, what about *Cube* (1997)? A film in which the environment itself is destructive but lacks the conscious existence needed to count as a being? Perhaps it's best to refer to horror like Supreme Court Justice Potter Stewart referred to hard-core pornography: "I know it when I see it." But, if genre is in the eye of the beholder, we cannot have a satisfactory definition of the horror genre. What if none of these are right? Or rather, what if none of these are wrong?

I purpose that the horror genre evolved out of the oral traditions of preliterate man and, in much the same way that playwriting has developed and evolved throughout human history since Aristotle's 'Poetics,' it has grown a set of tools, clichés, and storytelling devices through the cycle of innovation/repetition which we will explore more deeply below. Much like our earliest stories, tales of the horrific are primarily morality tales that serve to keep the values of the tribe/community alive by presenting the consequences of transgression.

As such, many of our earliest horror tales present a xenophobic outlook that presents outsiders as dangerous, without morals, or just plain evil; or, as deformed and destructive beings. The true purpose of art is to evoke an emotional effect—what better way to carry the message of the destructive nature of outsiders than through affective language and images. The Roman emperor Caligula took this to a new level—he made himself into the monster of the horror story, his famous quote reflects the controlling power of fear: "Let them hate me, so that they will but fear me."

To me, it is beyond doubt that the original purpose of horror stories was to control the value system and actions of the storyteller's tribal members. This would seem to match well with Carroll's idea of "art-horrified," in so much that the story is an art form, though the belief of these stories as true by the listeners serves to muddle a one-for-one analogue. Rather, "art-horror" could be said to have grown out of these stories, the same way the horror genre's plentiful deformed and destructive beings have (though those beings, as we'll see in the next chapter, still carry the power of metaphor). I propose that it is through an understanding of these definitions not as conclusive totalities within themselves but merely as components, which make up the modern day experience of the horror genre, that we find the truest definition of horror. Carroll, Ochoa, Grant, and even Stewart, in his own way, are all right, to various degrees, in their explanations of the horror genre— and, yet, they are all wrong.

The horror genre, as I have come to define it within my own thinking, is a part of an organically growing process of codifying our stories based on a set of storytelling devices. These devices are diverse and bountiful across the entirety of human storytelling but are easily recognizable within the framework of cinema. For example, a western is a genre that tends to feature open deserts, 'Mexican standoffs,' anti-heros, bandits, cattle farming, Native Americans, etc, ad infinitum—but one would not judge the lack of these devices as grounds to exclude a film such as *Meek's Cutoff* (2010) from being called a western.

It is in this way that the lack of physical effect required for Carroll's "art-horror" or the lack of Ochoa's deformed and destructive beings do not correspond to a film's disqualification as a work of horror. Rather, what Carroll and Ochoa have identified as horror are merely a part of the whole rather than the whole itself. A poorly made film may fail to affect the viewer but, through the use of the tools of horror storytelling, would still be clearly identifiable as existing within the confines of horror. Further, as these tools grow and evolve, the flexibility of the horror genre will be seen to grow—as evidenced by the existence of crossover genres such as Horror-Comedy and Sci-Fi-Horror. It is a recognition of these tropes, clichés, devices, and tools, that leads to this flexibility; as a fan watches more horror films, they understand horror films better and their exposure to these tools allows them to see how they have been bent (or, Scream Writers, how they *can* be bent) to expand on the knowledge and stories of our horrific forefathers.

Historical Trends

In order to understand the rise and "fall" of the horror genre—which, truthfully, has never been in the creative rut that bloggers would have you believe—we will be looking at what are called horror cycles.

A horror cycle is a period of horror film production that can be identified as sharing a common DNA. Horror isn't the only genre with a claim to a cyclical approach to production topics —for example, we can see it in the western genre (classic, revisionist, spaghetti); disco film; or even true event film (the slate of 9/11 films are a prime example). It is the horror genre that, while still producing films with bold new ideas throughout its 100+ year history, has embraced cyclical production practices to an almost obsessive degree.

By taking a quick look at the horror cycles of the past, we will have a better understanding of our place within the ongoing film history around us. In order to keep this section short, and of practical use, I have broken it into five sub-chapters. The first covers the birth of film, horror film as a genre, and brings us up to the 1960s; thus, it will cover the cycles to have been most strongly affected by censorship. Next we will be digging into the 1960s to look at how Herschell Gordon Lewis invented the gore film, George Romero reinvented the zombie, *Rosemary's Baby* (1968) brought Satan into the family, and how the decline of censorship was achieved by the end of the decade.

Blurring a straight forward chronological ordering of history, we will then look back at the Italian giallo film, its influence on the slasher film, as well as the cycles that further built off of the 1960s leading to the end of the 1980s. The slasher will give way to the post-modern slasher of the 1990s, the concurrent remake cycles of the 2000s, the post 9/11 rise of torture porn, and the invention of the found footage film. Finally, we'll close out with a look at recent trends to see what they can tell us about the future.

Pre-1960

Before the release of *Dracula* and *Frankenstein* (both 1931), there really wasn't an idea of "a horror film." *Dracula* was the first of the two to be released but the idea that it was the birth of a new genre was not immediately apparent; in fact, a heavy component of *Dracula*'s marketing was focused on promoting it as "the strangest love story ever told"—despite the fact that romance isn't a point of focus within the film. It wasn't until *Frankenstein* showed that the success of *Dracula* was no fluke that the genre was born. (This pattern of twists on storytelling techniques requiring a second successful film before forming a genre is an important feature to pay attention to.)

The first film with the successful twist is a **Pioneer Production** and requires a **Trailblazer Hit** to confirm the success of the sub/genre itself. For a deep discussion of this process and the many complications it can feature, check out Richard Nowell's *Blood Money: A History of the First Teen Slasher Film Cycle*.). Universal, as the studio that made both *Dracula* and *Frankenstein*, would go on to dominate this **Classical Horror Cycle**.

Despite the fact that the horror film didn't exist until Universal's monsters in the 1930s, many scholars actually place the first horror cycle a decade earlier and on another continent. A small selection of films came out of the post World War I Germany, a downtrodden country that discovered a new form of filmmaking: **German Expressionism**, a bold, new, and twisted approach to filmmaking that used its distorted mise-en-scène not strictly as the location of the plot's action, or the stage dressing, but as a projection of the warped psyches of the characters within. Many of the creatives involved in this cycle would find their way into Hollywood's Classical Horror Cycle of the 30s.

The Classical Horror Cycle burned itself out by the 1940s. This is perhaps due to the real life horrors of World War II, or perhaps to the strictures imposed on the genre by the **Motion Picture Production Code**, but it was here that the genre suffered its first "crisis." The films featuring the Universal monsters had fallen into parody, one of the key signs, for any subgenre, that the end times are near. However, every period of production that has been considered to mark the genre as dying has come to be fondly remembered. The horror genre merely disassembles itself with parody, when it becomes too repetitive, and rises stronger than ever like Jason Voorhees.

As the Universal monsters turned to parody, perhaps spending too much time with the likes of Abbott and Costello, RKO decided to launch its own line of horror productions and they hired **Val Lewton** to head it. Working officially as a producer, Lewton took a look at the low budgets he would have to work with and created a series of amazingly tense and gripping stories with a strong focus on atmosphere and character psychology. Given the era that these films were produced in and the titles they were given—such as *Cat People* (1942), *I Walked with a Zombie* (1943) and *The Curse of the Cat People* (1944)—it comes as a surprise to many modern viewers just how serious these films are. The titles were imposed on Lewton but otherwise he was given free reign—and because of that, we can look at the **Lewton Cycle** as the start of what we would now consider **Psychological Horror**.

By the 50s, monsters were making a comeback—only this time they were coming from outer space! Science fiction was big and it shared a lot of the same DNA as horror, which is why the **Science Fiction Cycle** was the most important cycle of the decade. But as far as straight horror? A small British company called Hammer Film Productions had been making films since 1935 but it wasn't until the company produced color adaptations of *The Curse of Frankenstein* (1957) and *Dracula* (1958) that the **Hammer Horror Cycle** was started. This cycle can be seen as part of a revival of the **Gothic Horror** style of the Classical Horror Cycle and the primary influence of Roger Corman's 1960s **Edgar Allen Poe Cycle**.

The decade might have been a lean one, with the major horror cycle not beginning until the decade was half over, but 1960 made it all worth it with the release of *Psycho*.

Blood, Brains and Babies: The 1960s and the Fall of Censorship

Hitchcock's *Psycho* had a profound effect on the future of the horror genre. But, as far as kicking off a horror cycle of its own, it had little immediate effect—we will see it have a more profoundly integral connection to the films of the next section. *Psycho*, much like the later *The Texas Chainsaw Massacre*, relied not on explicit blood and gore but rather on planting the suggestion of blood and gore within the minds of the audience. Gore had yet to truly find a way onto the big screen.

Enter Herschell Gordon Lewis aka The Grandfather of Gore. Lewis had his start in the "nudie cuties" and "roughies"—softcore skin flicks that either played as innocent (cuties) or battered a heavy hand across the face (roughies). As the market was bottoming out on these features, Lewis tried something that had never been done before. He made the **Gore Film**. The first was *Blood Feast* (1963) but this was soon followed with a trilogy. While Lewis' films did not spark off a horror cycle directly, they did introduce a staple of the genre—one that would rise to prominence as censorship was falling and the boundaries of "good taste" were being pushed. Lewis made his films outside of the studio system, he was a master of exploitation and knew he wouldn't be able to make *Blood Feast* through "proper" studios. The Motion Picture Production Code would never have allowed something so grotesque.

However, studio films were pushing the limits of what was acceptable as well. Nudity has had a long battle getting to the screen but, because of the art house movement, it was becoming more acceptable. Perhaps the best example of an early horror film pushing its subject matter, including a rape scene that is both explicit and a nightmare dreamscape, is *Rosemary's Baby*. Polanski's film would turn out to be a powerful calling card for the director, one that would influence a whole subgenre of **Occult Horror** (which we will be looking at closer below), but one that could have only come out of the era it was made. The Hays Code (as it was popularly called) was collapsing but it was still a restraint when Polanski was making *Rosemary's Baby*, one that strengthened the film rather than weakened it.

Released on June 12, 1968, *Rosemary's Baby* was released less than five months before the Motion Picture Production Code was scrapped in favour of the **MPAA (Motion Picture Association of America)** film rating system on November 1, 1968. The MPAA's system would classify films under G, M, R, or X: General; Mature; Restricted; or Sexually Explicit.

It's too bad, or perhaps it's just perfect, that the rating system was put in a month to the day after the most important horror film of the decade: George A. Romero's *Night of the Living Dead* (1968). Romero's film reinvented the **Zombie Film**. it showed the dead walk, attack, and eat the living in gruesome, graphic detail. Because the rating system was not yet in place, Roger Ebert was able to describe the theatre he first saw the movie in as having "maybe two dozen people in the audience who were over 16." The film, by all means, is a masterpiece—but it is a horrific, visceral masterpiece that clearly wasn't for children, as Ebert conveyed when he wrote "I don't think the younger kids really knew what hit them."

Is terrorizing kids the goal of the horror genre? Not exactly, the goal is to terrorize the audience and sometimes that audience is kids. Did they know what hit them? Not really. But hit them it did. Most importantly, it was one of the key films that pushed many of the kids in the direction of becoming the horror filmmakers of the next couple decades. For me, *The Evil Dead* pushed me in this direction; for them, they just had to spend a *Night of the Living Dead* scared out of their wits.

From the Giallo to the Slasher; or, Someone Call an Exorcist

The **Giallo** was a kind of murder mystery from Italy. They made little sense, most of the time, featured horrendously violent scenes of murder, often directed at women, and changed the future of the horror genre. They were called **Giallo** films because it means yellow and they were inspired by murder mystery novels that were given yellow covers when published in Italy. These often dream-like films tended *not* to concern themselves with the usual murder mystery questions— "Who is the killer?" or "How will they catch the killer?"—but rather they provoked the question: "What the hell is going on?" This purely Italian genre allowed filmmakers as varied and impressive as Mario Bava, Elio Petri, Sergio Martino, Dario Argento, and Lucio Fulci to produce their best works within its confines.

Perhaps the most well known of the horror subgenres and cycles is the **Slasher Film**. These films, perhaps the most formulaic of horror's output, focused on sexy teens, their bare bodies, the masked killers stalking them, and their death at the hands of the killer (typically with their bare hands, or some form of martial weapon). Freddy Krueger, Jason Voorhees, Michael Myers, Chucky, Ghostface, many of our favorite characters from horror history have come from the Slasher Film. These films can be seen as an extension of the Giallo and of Hitchcock's seminal *Psycho*. While these films may be seen as cheesy today, their legacy has yet to die and they continue to be explored with tweaks to the formula (or straight up attempts at shattering it).

Between the birth of the Giallo and the Slasher, we see the height of the Occult Film. *Rosemary's Baby* may have been the most important film of the 1960s, in regards to the Occult Film, but it was not until the massive success of *The Exorcist* (1973) that these films really came into their own. Considered by many to be the scariest film of all time, *The Exorcist* gave way to a plethora of imitators. However, it was not the rip-off artists that made this film so important but rather the fact that it showed the box office appeal (and our fear of) religiosity and the devil had over the cinema. It is because of the trail *The Exorcist* blazed that we have: *Satan's Slave* (1976); *The Devil's Rain* (1975); *To the Devil a Daughter* (1976); *The Omen* (1976); and *The Sentinel* (1977), to speak only of the films following immediately in its wake.

Finding Footage of Post-Modern Slashers Remaking Torture Porn

The Slasher Film lead to a proliferation of cheesy, formulaic sequels that focused not on pushing the boundaries of the genre—like the films of the 70s often tried to do—instead, much like '80s culture in general, the focus of the horror genre was on easily digestible popcorn flicks. These films might give the audience a start, push couples closer together, but no one was leaving the theatre feeling shook. As sequels gave way to diminishing box-office returns, a familiar rallying cry was heard: "The horror film is facing a crisis."

Of course, we've already seen that there is never so much a "crisis" as there is a "slow period" —and the 1990s, despite starting off slow, would come to a close, paving the way for the future ahead. The first of the '90s films to really shake up the system was *Scream* (1996); here was a film that was part parody and part slasher. Only the slasher elements were no longer fun but horrifically violent and the parody was now a self-reflection on the "rules" of the Slasher Film. But this time around it wasn't just the filmmakers that were aware of the rules—the characters knew them, too. *Scream* kicked off a string of **Teen Slashers** or, as I prefer to refer to them, **Post-Modern Slashers**. These were films that played with audience expectations and gave their characters the genre knowledge that horror fans had for years.

Only a few years later, one of the biggest movements in recent horror history began with a little film called *The Blair Witch Project*, a masterpiece on a small budget. The groundbreaking aspect of the film is easy to explain: the characters in the film are the characters holding the camera, therefore everything we see or hear is diegetic and filtered through the "reality" of the characters. By taking the camera from the "filmmakers" and giving it to the characters, *The Blair Witch Project*'s success (despite not being the first to stumble upon this concept) was the pioneer production that lead to the trailblazer hit *Paranormal Activity* (2007) to make **Found Footage Films** a staple of the genre.

On September 11, 2001, the world of American filmmaking was changed unexpectedly when terrorists flew planes into the World Trade Centre and caused the deaths of thousands of innocent people. It is in this charged environment that we see what has been labeled as **Torture Porn** come to prominence. Torture Porn is not pornography but rather a subgenre of horror films that focus their attention on the torture and dismemberment of the human body to levels of excess that parallel the excess of pornography. These films, despite being disparate in plot, share a level of gruesomeness that arose from attempts to make sense of the tragedy that had befallen the country.

Meanwhile, in a case of "now for something entirely different," following the success of *The Ring* (2002), a remake of a Japanese horror film from 1998 titled *Ringu*, a slate of films remaking Asian (though mostly Japanese) horror films could be seen as existing within an **Asian Remake Cycle**. These films introduced Western audiences to Eastern approaches of storytelling and fear making that was unlike anything the West had produced. This remake cycle existed concurrently with a more general **Remake Cycle** that would see updated versions of *The Omen* (2006), *Friday the 13th* (2009), *Halloween* (2007), *The Hills Have Eyes* (2006), *The Texas Chainsaw*

Massacre (2003), *My Bloody Valentine* (2009), and so, so, so many more. While the Asian Remake Cycle has mostly been dead in the water, the more general Remake Cycle is still going strong with news of a *Child's Play* (1988) remake having just been announced earlier in the morning that I am writing this.

What Sights the Future Holds

The most recent of film cycles, at the point of writing, would appear to be a return to **Supernatural Horror**, a reprieve from the horrors of reality that Torture Porn had so lovingly focused on. Films like *The Conjuring* (2013), *Insidious* (2010), *Annabelle* (2014), and *It* (2017) all place the cause of horror in the hands of the supernatural rather than the human. The success of *The Conjuring* series was great enough to spin off into two *Annabelle* films and *The Nun* (2018), all of which have been put into a "shared universe"—the newest of inventions within the film world, taken from the model of the Marvel films.

Shared universes may seem wonderful to some—those who've drank the Kool-Aid, so to speak—or terrible to others—those that are too far behind the times, some might say. Shared universes are a double edged sword: creating a universe keeps fans coming back for more but it also leads to fatigue, there being just so much stuff you have to know and keep up on or you risk falling behind. *The Conjuring* seems to have found success in this model but one doesn't have to look very far to see the casualties along the way (just look at how quickly *The Dark Universe* was wiped off the Internet following the failure of 2017's *The Mummy*).

Despite this push towards creating a universe, the independent horror scene has continued to pump out original, thought provoking, stand alone films like *The VVitch* (2015), *The Babadook* (2014), *Starry Eyes* (2014), *Tenemos la Carne* (*We Are The Flesh*, 2016), *The Devil's Candy* (2015), *The Neon Demon* (2016), and *Raw* (2016), just to name a few of my personal favorites. Many of these films may fall under seemingly straightforward subgenres but each has found a unique way of telling their stories and of pushing the horror film into new, untold depths.

Whether you're aiming for big budget studio horror, or small and personal independent scares, by paying attention to where the genre has been you can find new ways to explore old ideas, identify emerging trends, and craft stories that continue the horrific legacy you've come here to join.

Subgenres

We've already touched on several subgenres above but not nearly all of them. What comes first, the subgenre or the movie? It's a tricky question, honestly. Subgenres arise when a connection can be ascertained between several films and labeled. So subgenres arise out of the grouping of films and for them to exist the films have to exist first. However, once a subgenre exists, knowledge of the subgenre affects how films that fit within it will be received and processed by audiences in various degrees depending on the individual's previous subgeneric knowledge. Then, being built on the shoulders of murderers, the new story will become a part of the wider subgeneric conversation.

Do you have to think about all of that? No, not really. The important part is to have an understanding of the competition of your story—think of your story as a book proposal: What are the texts that have been written on the subject? Why is this one unique? If you think of it in these terms you can find ways to twist established conventions, fuse subgenres together and see what happens, or, if you're really lucky, discover an entirely new subgenre!

If you're the type—like me—that gets caught up wanting to know the ins and outs of every subgenre, then *Horror Films by Subgenre: A Viewer's Guide* by Chris Vander Kaay & Kathleen Fernandez-Vander Kaay is a must read; the book covers more than 70 subgenres of the horror film. However, let me stress that a comprehensive knowledge of every subgenre is not required to be a good Scream Writer. Some genres you just won't care for, others you might not even consider to be a subgenre and, perhaps the most surprising of all, sometimes a lack of knowledge on what should and shouldn't be in a film of the subgenre you choose can actually be a benefit. But, for those of you like me (obsessed with learning as much as you can about this wonderful genre and crafting stories inside of it) the Vander Kaays' book is an absolute treasure trove.

Further Study

As well as the Vander Kaay's book mentioned above, for more information on the history of the horror genre I would recommend watching *A History of Horror with Mark Gatiss* (2010) and Bravo's *The 100 Scariest Movie Moments* (2004). For those that are interested in figuring out which films are worth watching, *Horror! 333 Films to Scare You to Death* by James Marriott and Kim Newman offers a solid grounding covering the silent era through to the early 2010s. For those with an account on the film-centered social media platform Letterboxd, I can be found under the username Horrordaily and have been running a history of horror film challenge for three years now. In the challenge I set out 52 categories, for a film a week, in which participants create a list of 52 movies they'll watch over the year. It is called the History of Horror challenge because its goal is to show a progression over time and to cover various subgenres, movements, directors, actors, national film industries, and the like so as to help the participants gain a fuller understanding of horror film history while having a blast and see what others are watching.

Chapter 2: Monsters

I love monsters the way people worship holy images. To me, they really connect in a very fundamental way to my identity.

Guillermo del Toro

When we looked at the definition of the horror genre, we saw that Ochoa's *Deformed and Destructive Beings: The Purpose of Horror Films* thinks the genre exists just to show monsters. That sounds too limiting but I do think that the title sums up monsters quite well. Monsters are those things that are disgusting to look at, they are abject in sight. But while we may pity the Elephant Man for being abject in appearance, we do not consider him to be a monster. It takes more than just deformity to be a monster. Monsters require a destructive nature. Monsters are the dangerous abject.

Monsters come in all forms, including humans. Human monsters may not be abject to look upon, at least not in the same way that the zombified abomination of flesh and gore that Aunt Ruth turned into is abject, but how can one not speak of the evil of men like Ted Bundy, Jeffrey Dahmer, or Albert Fish as being anything other than monstrous? The deformity of *Deformed and Destructive Beings* does not limit itself to the physical realm but rather takes into account deformity of the mind—something that psychological horror films love to explore—and positions the serial killer, or whichever form the evil of humanity took, as every bit as monstrous as Bigfoot, Freddy Krueger, or *The Thing* (1982).

Perhaps no film better explores the contrast between physical and mental deformity than Clive Barker's *Nightbreed* (1990). In a film populated with a plethora of strange and intriguing, sometimes frightening, "monsters," the scariest and most inhumane of the characters is that played by Body Horror filmmaker extraordinaire, David Cronenberg. Cronenberg's Dr. Decker is a very human monster. He hides his perfect normal face behind a mask while he murders and tortures innocent people. Yet, despite his The Stranger Next Door good looks, when compared to the deformed creatures of Midian, Decker is a monster of unparalleled proportions—enough so that one is forgiven for turning against their fellow humans.

Many horror films rely on a monster, Ochoa is correct in this; however, such films as *La rose de fer* (*The Iron Rose*, 1973) and *The Changeling* (1980) are examples of films without monsters. These are films that rely on atmosphere and mood to impart chills, two elements that we will be looking at in more detail in the next chapter. However, these are much fewer and farther between when one considers the sheer number of movie monsters the horror genre has produced.

We love monsters. We love monsters so much that they're not even stuck in the horror genre. Monsters have been an intricate part of our history as any lover of mythology already knows. Putting aside the historical lure of monsters, our 21st century could easily be described as overrun by them. Pop culture hits like *Star Wars* (1977), *Jurassic World* (2015), even superhero films like *Batman Begins* (2005) and *The Dark Knight* (2008)—each gives screentime to monsters.

And we love it.

It's not just the silver screen either, with television shows like *Buffy the Vampire Slayer* (1996-2003), *Stranger Things* (2016-), and (perhaps too on the nose?) *Aaahh!!! Real Monsters* (1994-1997). Even at home, we want to spend our time with fiends.

There are many reasons for us to love monsters—they're cool looking, powerful, *other*—and in this chapter we will explore these reasons alongside discussions about designing them, revealing them in your screenplays and more. But before we get into writing and designing our creeps, let's take a moment to realize how powerful the meanings of monsters are.

The Power of Monsters as Metaphors

Rare is the movie where the monster is just a monster. Monsters lend themselves to metaphor in a way that is more direct and noticeable than damn near any other element of film and storytelling. In recent years we have seen a plethora of pop culture articles that have claimed some variation of the same story: "The Thinking Man's

Horror Movie is Here." However, monsters show us that horror has always been the domain of the thinking man; a monster is rarely just a monster, after all—something that the popular consciousness is catching on to.

Monsters don't exist—though don't tell that to the giant squid or the platypus, two cryptozoological myths that were proven real—and it is this fact of non-existence that allows the monster to serve as metaphor. A film about a serial killer may be less metaphorical, generally, but the human monster can also be used metaphorically, even though they do exist. Serial killer films tend to look at "the big picture," that is to say that often the point that they are trying to make is similar to the monster film but instead of focusing that point through the monster, they focus the point through the situation that allowed for the monster (e.g. a film can indict familial bounds for producing the killer, such as in *Psycho*, *Snowtown* (2011), or *Henry: Portrait of a Serial Killer* (1986); or it can point the blame at law enforcement and the legal system, *10 Rillington Place* (1971) is a perfect example of this; mental illness and our handling of it; or even the scariest indictment of all … pure incomprehensible evil; *Halloween* (1978) is a perfect example of this but *Henry* also could be argued to fit this description depending on one's interpretation of Henry's life story as either true or false). But the monsters that don't exist—or, again, thinking of the platypus, those we hope and pray don't exist—are creeping, crawling, bloodthirsty metaphors and, as we shall see, their position of metaphoric power is a double edged sword that we must be careful when wielding.

How about a few examples? Frankenstein's Monster, from the 1931 Universal version, has been put forth as an example of: a motherless child; the means through which to triangulate the homosexual desires of his creator; an indictment of eugenics; a symbol of man encroaching on God's domain, and so much more you could fill a book with it (and, in fact, several people already have). The deranged killers of *The Hills Have Eyes* (1977) and *The Texas Chainsaw Massacre*, according to Robin Wood, can be read as a repressed proletariat striking back against the bourgeois. The rape scene in *Deliverance* (1972)—which is not a monster but can be seen as a monsterous action, the backwoods characters committing the heinous deed are as other as can be for our city-slicking protagonists—has been read along similar lines. It, from *It Follows* (2014), is a stand-in for sexually transmitted diseases and, following along those lines, don't even get me started on endless lineup of monsters that represent female sexuality (primarily seen through the male gaze and thus representing male fears of female sexuality rather than female sexuality in a vacuum). This list could go on and on but I trust that you are starting to get the picture—monsters are rarely just monsters.

If monsters are metaphors, does that mean you have to know what your monster stands for right away? Absolutely not! As you develop your story/monster, the meaning of the monster will evolve and grow and, if you pay attention, you can start to understand what it is the monster is saying. Some creatives start with what the monster means and work backwards from there, some find it while they are building it, and others, yet, don't discover it at all (think of *Friday the 13th* (1980) and how it was written with the goal of copying *Halloween* rather than saying anything of its own). However, even if you haven't thought of or discovered the meaning of your monster by the time the script is out of your hands, audiences will have their own interpretation as to the meaning of what the monster stands in for metaphorically.

Because audiences bring their own meaning, we as humans are prone to discovering patterns of meaning, I believe that it is important to at least think through the possible interpretations that could be read; the worst possible outcome is you create a story that metaphorically feeds on ideas of misogyny, racism, homophobia, or any other form of hatred. Perhaps you are specifically feeding in these ideas, in which case, please just stop writing now—we have enough hatred in the world. But there is nothing worse than realizing that your story is being viewed as primarily fuelled by these kinds of negative emotions.

Because the monster is a metaphor, the monster is powerful—and not just because it bleeds acid, destroys minds, or rends flesh.

<u>Designing Your Fiends</u>

In this section, we will be looking at how to build our monsters. In order to play the role of Dr. Frankenstein, we will explore how the ecology and biology of monsters is connected; examine monster movie case studies to discover the origins of several key monsters and how we can learn from them to improve and inspire our own ghouls; we'll discover their weaknesses so our heroes can stand a fighting chance; investigate the supernatural be it ghost or magick; and we'll take time out to explore the psychology and "origins" of human monsters, through further case studies.

It's important to note that not every monster requires an answer to every section we'll be looking at; for example, some origins are never explained—this can be due to an oversight on the writers part but more often than not it is due to the very simple fact that the unknown is frightening and revealing the origin only serves to lesson this quality. Similarly, there are creatures such as Godzilla, Mothra, and the rest of our oversized kaiju buddies that could not exist within our world; that is to say, if they were to exist in the real world, their biology would kill them off before they were ever a problem to us. In fact, creatures only as large as an elephant cannot withstand a fall of a dozen feet let alone the kind of pummelling a kaiju takes. Because horror exists within the fantastique, it does not need to conform to the rules of our world if it doesn't want to.

However, the magick, supernatural, and otherworldly aspects of horror only cover themselves—when we bring mad science into the picture, or even just realism, we have to think about our monsters in a far more grounded approach.

You can read this section in its entirety or, as you find it applies to your current script, browse the relevant sections. This chapter will close out with a discussion on revealing our monsters and the descriptive language we use to bring them to life.

Origins

I've just mentioned that not every monster's origins need to be explained, yet I'm going to slightly contradict myself—on the next page even, the nerve! The origin of the monster may not be explained, in and of itself, but the origin of the monster within the story has to be explained. This is to say that your monsters have to come from somewhere—yes, perhaps they come from an unknown dimension that you're not even sure about; however, they came from that unknown to be within the physical space that the characters and action of your story is set in, so how did they get there? Perhaps they were stuck, dormant for centuries, and have now been awakened due to fracking. Or, perhaps our characters are the ones that wandered in the monster's space; it is this origin that I refer when I say the origin within the story. This origin is tied not to the birth of the monster but to its place the story that you are writing and, as such, we will be dealing further with this when we discuss plots.

Here we are concerned with the birth of our monsters, which may not have been "born" at all. Perhaps your monsters were made by science—oh the vanity of mankind, they thought they could play God and take life into their own hands. The most famous of science-birthed monstrosities is, of course, Frankenstein's Monster, that lumbering patchwork abomination. It's not hard to see a "be careful what you wish for" theme emerge from Shelley's foundational text, nor is it hard to see how those themes have found themselves at the forefront of subsequent "science-gone-awry" narratives. *Godzilla* (1954) is often thought to be the product of nuclear radiation; though this is incorrect, it was underwater hydrogen bomb tests that awoke this creature of pure destruction—it took mankind's destructive ambitions and gave them form. Similarly, the wonderfully campy *Them!* (1954) does actually locate the origin of its over-sized—though adorable—ants as a direct result of nuclear radiation. Hell, even *Jurassic Park* (1993) places the blame for the events of the film at the hands of science—it's not that dinosaurs are terrifying killing machines, it's man's attempt to play God that is to blame, not his creations.

Like the pieces that Dr. Frankenstein used to build his monster, the monster of science is often innocent before the scientist meddles with it. The ants of *Them*, the dinosaurs (dead so long, no harm to anyone) of *Jurassic Park*, the *Tarantula!* (1955), all animals without morality that have been mutated (or resurrected) through science—they have simple instincts that govern their lives but because of science those instincts are now a threat to man. But it's not always innocent animals that find themselves perverted at the hands of science. *I was a Teenage Frankenstein* (1957) and *La Horripilante Bestia Humana* (*Night of the Bloody Apes*, 1969) are two examples of science-based horror in which the mad scientists test out their experiments on innocent subjects. These two cases are examples of truly mad scientists, but scientists that mean good have also found themselves caught up in monster generating experiments; though often if the scientist is of moral character, they will experiment on themselves rather than another.

Not all science-gone-awry monsters are torn from the natural world. Sometimes it is our attempts to make the world a better place that come back to haunt us. The creatures from *I Am Legend* (2007) spring not from an attempt to weaponism science but rather from an attempt to cure cancer. Are the viruses from *Contagion* (2011) or *The Stand* (1994) monsters? They wreck havoc and destruction on those they touch, they are deformed and destructive beings (of the smallest order, putting the *Gremlins* (1984) to shame). If so, we have science to thank for these.

While *I Am Legend* demonstrates a new world order of monsters that have arisen out of disease, *The Return of the*

Living Dead (1985) is a perfect example of disease giving birth to a classic monster, the zombie. Though never explicitly putting the blame on science, it is the army's incapability of dealing with an outbreak of zombies—in the lore of the film, the zombies are what inspired Romero to film *Night of the Living Dead*—that gives way to the outbreak we witness in the film. These zombies can be seen as fitting in with our monsters spawned of disease or contagion—they continue to be a contagion, in that their bite spreads their sickness, while also being a physical threat that our heroes must fight or flee. In this way, zombies are given an origin of science—though not always man made.

Horror is also ripe with fiends that warn us to "Watch the skies!" If you want an easy origin for your monster, one that immediately mutes the question of "How can it exist?" then locate your creature's origin in outer space. We don't know what's out there, anything can be out there—in fact, perhaps what's out there is *The Thing*. Our shapeshifting, formless, nameless entity could not exist on this planet—it truly is as alien as can be and can only be accepted as coming from space. But space monsters don't always need to be quite so elusive to understand; *Critters* (1986) gives us space aliens that look like the oversized offspring of a rat and a porcupine. If it wasn't for their ability to pilot spacecraft, speak (F**K!!) and plan traps, we might confuse them as just another of the native monstrosities that call Australia home. Hell, your space monsters don't even need to look like monsters—perhaps they look like just *Killer Klowns from Outer Space* (1988).

Speaking of Australia, let's take a look at the monsters of the natural world such as those in *Jaws* (1975), *Razorback* (1984), *Orca* (1977), or even *Long Weekend* (1978). *Jaws* and *Orca* explore those creatures that call the depths of the sea their home—what more do you need to tell us? We already know that they are powerful killing machines, alien to us, designed to murder anything that get their paths. They are monsters that exist already. *Razorback* posits a giant razorback boar as its monster, and never attempts to truly explain its origin; it is a freak of nature. *Prophecy* (1979) combines its creatures origins: on the one hand, it is a natural horror, a bear already serving as a terrifying creature (as any Vancouverite would agree); on the other hand, it is the fault of science—it is the result of a fungicide being used illegally by the loggers of the film. However, it is also hinted at that the creature is Katahdin, a vengeful spirit of the forest, which brings us to our next kind of origin: the supernatural.

I am going to combine the terms supernatural and demonic; while the two refer to different entities (the latter requiring some acknowledgement of an Abrahamic religion), they are also often conflated with each other. The film *Insidious*, for example, sets itself up first as a haunted house film, transitions into a haunted child film, then reveals that the main antagonist is not a spirit but a demon (while also having plenty of ghosts within the 100 minute runtime). *Insidious* says that these spirits and demons come from a place called The Further, and then washes its hands of any more elaborating.

Other films such as *The Exorcist* see their demons as random occurrences in the battle between Good and Evil, God and Devil. *The Exorcist* also hints that perhaps Regan has invited this possession onto herself when the film teases the idea that an ouija board might have been involved. Even though the ouija board only became a thing through the spiritualist fade in the 1890s and is thought to be nothing more than an example of the ideomotor reflex, we attribute power to these boards. They are an attempt to touch the other side and, much like the playing God we see in science-gone-awry films, we accept the idea that there were things that mankind was not supposed to meddle in. We have seen ouija boards be the origin of supernatural origin before—could there be any more perfect example than *Ouija* (2014) and *Ouija: Origin of Evil* (2016)? But they are far from the only supernatural origin that we readily accept. How many ghosts have we seen as a result of someone dying with unfinished business? How many ghosts, like those of *Poltergeist* (1982), have we seen return because they've had their eternal slumber disturbed?

Let's not forget the other wonderful facet of the supernatural that is magick. Magick, as an origin for monsters rather than the monster itself (such as witches), is an easy way to explain the origin of a monster. *Pumpkinhead* (1988) was conjured by a witch to get revenge, on behalf of Ed Harley, against those that accidentally killed the man's son. An elderly witch and warlock use their magick to breathe life into the toys from *Dolls* (1987). Even *Rosemary's Baby* uses magick, of a demonic nature, to spawn the titular monster (though the film's horror arises out of the conspiracy to birth the devil's child rather than the child itself). When magick is used to spawn a monster, the monster will have limitations that are often separated from the magick itself. The toys of *Dolls* can be smashed and broken, for example, so magick monsters stand apart from the magick users that we will explore later on within this chapter.

It may seem like the origin of your monster could be … anything! With limitless options, there is the possibility for limitless indecisiveness and that's not good. Let's wrap up our discussion on origins by exploring what links these different origins together. From the supernatural to the natural and from science to space, their similarities might not be readily apparent but they are there.

The most readily apparent of these similarities is the **otherness** of the monsters. Science spawned monsters are creatures that wouldn't have existed if not for the folly of man; space monsters are other to the nth degree; our supernatural beings come from another plane of existence; … but surely *Jaws* and *Orca* are natural. However, both of these films go out of their way to stress the difference of their monsters. *Jaws* makes sure that you realize the shark on the loose is bigger than normal, while *Orca* bestows a level of intelligence to its whale that is ludicrous (but just so damn fun). Okay but what about a film like *Squirm* (1976) or *Slugs* (1988) or *Arachnophobia* (1990) or *Ticks* (1993) or, or, or, ... These films often do stress the odd behaviour of their creatures in order to play on our natural fear of *the other* but they also serve to demonstrate another ancient human fear: the abject.

While the *Oxford English Dictionary* describes the abject as an adjective that means:

1.   (of something bad) experienced or present to the maximum degree.
1.1.   (of a situation or condition) extremely unpleasant and degrading.

The definition which best serves our purpose is that proposed by Julia Kristeva in *Powers of Horror*, where she describes the abject (specifically, the reaction of abjection) as a threatened breakdown in the distinction between the self and the other. This breakdown can best be reflected in the corpse: it was once human, now it is not; I am living now but in the future I will be a corpse; the body is whole, now it is rotting and decaying. However, this breakdown does not necessarily refer to those things that are physically breaking down—the subject believes the universe is one of a loving God, so John Carpenter's *Prince of Darkness* (1987) threatens this belief, it causes abjection in the viewer. Because monsters should not be, they are abject; because we are disgusted by garbage and insects, we consider them to be abject. If you locate your monsters origin within the abject, you are already causing the audience disgust and horror—our main goal as Scream Writers.

What should not be but is; what we don't understand; what disgusts us; what we consider as Other. These are what scare us. If we use these in the creation of our monsters, not just in their descriptions and actions, then we have taken steps towards creating monsters that truly scare our audience and not just when our protagonists are in danger but on a deeper level, a level that will follow them out of the theatres.

The Origin of Human Evil

Much like the origins of the creatures we discussed above, the origins of human monsters don't always need to be explained. Think of a film like *Henry: Portrait of a Serial Killer*. We are given hints as to why Henry is the way he is, but the true terror of the film comes in the fact that he is just pure evil. The film plays with our sympathies towards Henry by offsetting him against the character of Otis and by developing a blooming romance between Henry and Otis' sister, Becky.

 Otis appears to us to be the more evil of the two: despite being brought into the serial killing lifestyle by Henry, Otis's attempts to rape his sister, his willingness to engage in acts of necrophilia, his attempts to molest high school children, even his part time job dealing drugs all position him as the true portrait of evil. As Henry and Becky become closer with one another, we see her as the beacon of hope that will lift Henry out of his evil ways. This is why the end of the film is such a shock when we realize what happened to Becky. Henry was, as the film has been subtly telling us, unknown—he was never truly understood by Becky or Otis or, most disturbingly yet, by us.

Henry does give clues as to what causes his evil. We are told that his mother was an evil woman, that Henry killed her because of her wickedness; and we see Henry's sexual repression when he murders the prostitute and again later when he berates Otis's necrophilia. So that's it then, Henry is the way he is because of sexual repression. Case closed. Or … is it? The murder of Becky at the end of the film shows us that we've never really understood Henry; and what's more, we're shown that Henry can't keep his story of how he killed his mother straight. This is a man that can't even keep track of his own lies, a man that avoids our every attempt to see inside his mind—all the hints that we are given can just as easily be red herrings. Henry is an example of **The Unknowable Killer**.

While technically you could include Michael Myers under the category of Unknowable Killer, *Halloween* reinforces the idea that Myers is not just an insane killer on the loose—he is pure evil through and through. From the devil's eyes, to his ability to shrug off half a dozen bullets, Myers stops being human by the end of the film—he's only unknowable until we realize that Dr. Loomis has been correct this whole time. We're never told why he kills his sister at the beginning of the film—at least, not until the sequels—but this traumatic event situated in the past is the key to understanding the vast majority of human monsters. *Psycho*, having been inspired by real life monster Ed Gein, does not get very deep into what it is that causes Norman Bates to go insane except to situate it around his relationship with his domineering mother.

Scream, also not digging overly deep, places the inciting incident of Billy's killing spree at the trauma surrounding Sidney's mother's affair with his father—an affair which caused Billy's mother to split, though that doesn't get into Stu's motivation at all. *Saw* (2004) locates Jigsaw's failed suicide attempt at the turning point in his decision to murder people who don't appreciate life. Again and again, the past rises to the surface in the form of violence within the serial killer film.

Another popular origin for filmic serial killers—as well as one we see far too often in reality—is the **Perfect Storm Relationship**. *Badlands* (1973), *Snowtown*, *Natural Born Killers* (1994), *Blood and Black Lace* (1964), Otis from *Henry: Portrait of a Serial Killer*, *The Honeymoon Killers* (1970), *The Hillside Strangler* (2004), *Mais ne nous délivrez pas du mal* (*Don't Deliver Us from Evil*, 1971) and *Heavenly Creatures* (1994) all present a pair of serial killers with the suggestion, either implicit or subtly, that they would not have sunk to the depths of murder and mayhem if it weren't for finding of each other. These are films that suggest that some people are just made for each other and it doesn't always mean a storybook Disney princess ending.

As is often true of real life killer couples, there tends to be a power imbalance within the killer couple; that is, one of the killers tends to dominate the action of the couple or the group. *Snowtown* presents a charismatic personality which ends up leading a cult of killers; *Badlands* shows that Martin Sheen's Kit leads while Sissy Spacek's Holly follows; Henry is in charge of Otis, as much as it pisses Otis off. However, this power dynamic can also be played with—one of the couple appears to be in charge but is being lead by the other/rest, as is the case with *Somos lo que hay* (*We Are What We Are*, 2010) in which the surviving member of the cannibalistic family is made to seem innocent for the cops despite the fact that she had dominated her brothers throughout the rest of the film.

Whereas the origins of our monsters had their roots located in The Other, our human monsters only really touch on The Other when they are The Unknowable Killer; otherwise, human monsters are typically located within sociological or psychological origins that either arise from their pasts or from the hand they have been dealt in life—a hand that gives them no other choice, such as Aileen Wuornos in *Monster* (2003). From time to time there are films that locate the killer's origins within a supernatural event such as *Frailty* (2001) or *Identity* (2003, a film which could claim a psychological origin but approaches its psychology so outlandishly that it could only be called supernatural).

These films have less in common with the straight serial killer narrative than they do with films, like *Candyman* (1992) or *Child's Play,* which include serial killers so far removed from reality as to become the fantasque. There are a few films, such as *Summer of Sam* (1999) and *Orphan* (2009), which collapse the barrier between the supernatural and the psychological in fascinating ways—the unreliable narrator, the hidden identity, these are films that focus less on the origin than on the twist reveal (well, *Summer of Sam*'s inclusion of supernatural elements aren't a twist as much as they are a reflection of the insanity of the main character—an insanity pulled straight out of real life).

In constructing your serial killers, your human monsters, look for those events in their lives that primed them for the murderous road. Then, look for the event within the story that triggers their killings, now that they've been primed. In *Scream*, the event in the past is the murder of Sidney's mother, the trigger in the present is the one year anniversary. *Henry* starts in medias res, though it does make suggestions as to a past that has primed Henry for the life he now lives (even if those suggestions are untrustworthy).

Even *Halloween*, with its Unknowable Killer, shows us his murder in the past (the primer), though it offers no suggestion as to the trigger for the killing spree he embarks on later. Understanding these two key events within your human monsters life will allow you to shape a killer that the audience understands—that's not to say they relate to but, rather, that they can fathom their actions given the circumstances. And, as with anything, understand that you can break and twist these elements—as long as you know why you're doing it!

But be careful, the origin of your human monsters' behaviour can easily come across poorly. For example, Jeffrey Dahmer was a homosexual and his sexual preference did play into his overall psychology. If you chose to pinpoint only the homosexuality, that would come across as placing blame on homosexuality itself and that would be absolute bullshit—we know that being a homosexual doesn't make you a serial killer. Within a storytelling perspective, it would be weak and trite. Within a humane perspective, it would be disgusting and fear mongering. The origin has power because the origin is another part of the overall metaphor.

And this doesn't just go for serial killers. If you are showing mental health issues as monstrous, please do your best to give dimension and understanding to the diseases that you are using to craft your antagonists. In fact, some of the most profoundly disturbing films don't focus on making a monster through mental health disorders but actually use the disorder as the monster: *Spider* (2002) and *Clean, Shaven* (1993) are two examples that look at the monstrosity of being human and sick. I'm not saying *not* to use mental illness in film but to take the time to understand what it is you're using; there are a lot of suffering people out there that don't need another film demonizing their struggles.

Ecology and Biology

When it comes to monsters of supernatural or extraterrestrial origin, their biology doesn't need to make logical sense—its very existence is already a transgression of the laws of our reality and, therefore, they are under no obligation to conform to modern science. However, if you locate your monsters origins within the realm of evolution (as many horror films have) then it is important to pay attention to the intricate link between ecology and biology. In order to explore this relationship, let's turn our attention to case studies of *The Descent* (2005), *Tremors* (1990) and *Mimic* (1997).

Tremors is a film about a small town, population 16, that comes under attack by a previously undiscovered species of underground creatures that get named graboids. Graboids are worm-like creatures with unknown origins (at least in the first film) but with a biology that makes perfect evolutionary sense considering their habitat. In fact, the first film cares so little about the origins of the creatures that it suggests: they came from outer space; they're from the far, far distant past; they're the result of genetic engineering; or they're the result of nuclear radiation. Whatever their origin, what matters to the film is that they are here now.

But what matters to us is their physiology.

The graboids of *Tremors* are giant carnivorous worms. They live underground so they've never evolved to have eyes because they never had reason for sight. In order to track their prey, graboids rely on seismic vibrations such as sounds and movement to locate their above ground meal. The head of a graboid ends in a pointed beak that helps to dislocate dirt and push it to the side of their massive bodies, while hardened setae (a monsterized version of the little hairs that earthworms have) work to push the graboids forward through the earth. The graboids also have a set of prehensile tongues that they use to scout above the ground and pull under any tasty food.

As the series went on the graboids were seen to evolve but each form that they took after their initial worm-like form would lack the ecological/biological thought that went into their first appearance. The graboids were approached first as a creature that has to exist, rather than just an interesting monster. And what came out of this focus on practical existence? *Tremors* is a wonderfully fun film that sets up a problem—giant worm monsters—and allows its characters to deal with the threat using science and logic to figure a way out of the situation. Because the creatures adhere to the laws of evolutionary biology, our characters are able to figure out that they can't see, figure out how they hunt, and they are then able to use this information to stay alive and beat the threat. A monster built from scientifically sound principles is not any less scary than a monster whose existence makes no sense—in fact, oftentimes they are scarier.

Neil Marshall's 2005 film *The Descent* follows a group of adrenaline junkie women that get together every so often to go whitewater rafting, cave diving, etc. We join them as they explore a cave that isn't listed on any map, get lost in the dark tunnels and have to work together to find a way out. This already horrifying experience of claustrophobia is complicated when they discover that they are not alone in the caves—there's some kind of humanoid monsters and our characters have the extreme misfortune of trespassing upon their territory.

The crawlers, as they were referred to by the production crew, are a kind of cavemen; they may have once been human—or, at least, of the homo genus—but their evolution diverged significantly due to their retreat into the caves. Like the graboids, the crawlers have no need for eyesight and, as such, they are completely blind. Instead, the crawlers rely on sound and smell in order to hunt their prey. Being that they are cave dwellers, they don't stand upright but move in a hunched over fashion—they crawl.

Not only has their posture evolved over the centuries in order to allow them to strive in a cave system, but they have also become adept climbers and demonstrate their agility by scaling impossibly steep walls. Unlike their human cousins, the crawlers have not formed a culture as far as we the viewer are aware. However, these creatures do have a primitive form of society that we only ever see allusions towards. Marshall was able to imbue his monsters with a sense of realism by including women and children within their ranks, an oversight that many horror films have made and which have left viewers scratching their heads—without women there isn't procreation, without children there aren't future generations.

In contrast to *Tremors* and *The Descent*, we have Guillermo Del Toro's *Mimic*. In New York, children are being infected with a deadly disease by cockroaches. Entomologist Dr. Susan Tyler genetically modifies a new breed of cockroaches which she christens the "Judas" breed. This need bug releases an enzyme which accelerates the metabolism of cockroaches so that they are unable to feed quick enough to avoid starvation. However, three years later, despite designing the Judas breed to be incapable of mating, they have continued to grow and strive and are now a threat facing the residents of the city that never sleeps.

Mimic presents an interesting adaptation of biology to fit ecology but fails to deliver it in a manner that is in any way believable. Being that these roaches live in New York, they are constantly surrounded by humans and so, like many species of bug, they adapt a camouflage strategy: they have grown to such a large size that they are able to wrap their "arms" around themselves to take on the appearance of a man in a trenchcoat. This wonderful effect, as mesmerizing as it is, is chilling. The thought of cockroaches the size of men with the capability to blend in among us is terrifying (and has been the plot of horror and comedies alike, ala *Meet the Applegates* (1990), *Arachnid* (2001), and 1988's *The Nest*). However, the film hand-waves over some important elements that are required to maintain the audience's suspension of disbelief.

We are asked to accept the idea that an accelerated metabolism is the root cause of the Judas breed's adaptation. However, metabolism does not equate to evolutionary growth. It took millions of years for the cockroach to evolve, as they date their existence back to at least the Carboniferous period of the Paleozoic era. However, within three years (only a few tens of thousands of generations of Judas cockroaches) we are expected to believe that these pests went from the size of a normal cockroach to the size of a fully grown adult male. To be blunt, it's complete bullshit.

This is not to say that the movie is bad; *Mimic* has its flaws (a complete disregard of scientific principles being one) but it still stands as an enjoyable little creature feature. I use it as a negative example because the film itself goes out of its way to bring science into the fold, while completely treading all over its own believability. As with any of the sections in Designing Your Fiends, exploring their link between ecology and biology is optional. But if you're going to act like you're interested in exploring it, you better make sure you do it right!

<u>The Supernatural</u>

We discussed the origins of the supernatural—conversing through a ouija board, dying with unfinished business, etc.—so here we will be less concerned with origin and focus more on an understanding of how the supernatural has been used within the horror film. Unlike monsters of material existence, the supernatural is positioned as being from another plane of existence. They may always be there but unnoticed (such as in 1990's *Ghost* or 1987's *From Beyond*) or they may be able to manifest within our reality due to their unfinished business (like 1987's *Prison* or 2004's *Shutter*); perhaps they can only be seen by those blessed/cursed with the sight (1999's *The Sixth Sense* or 2002's *The Eye*), or maybe it's they're stuck in a location (1980's *The Shining* or 1972's *The Stone Tape*). Hell, maybe the lines between supernatural occurrence and psychological happenings are so blurred they confuse the audience like in *Requiem* (2006), *Ich seh, Ich seh* (*Goodnight Mommy*, 2014), *Session 9* (2001), or *The Innocents* (1961).

With so many different representations of the supernatural—we didn't even get into vampires, werewolves, or your resurrected Jason Voorhees-type zombies—it might be easy to look at the supernatural as an anything goes approach to horror and figure that it means you don't have to be as diligent with the supernatural as you would be otherwise. However, let's not trick ourselves into a bad attitude. The supernatural requires just as much work, if not more, than any other form of horror antagonist because the importance of rules is magnified tenfold when dealing with the supernatural.

What do I mean by rules?

To answer that question, let's look first as a previously discussed monster: the graboid. Because the graboid is not supernatural in origin, we know that they abide by the rules of our reality. They don't have eyes, they hunt with sound and vibrations, so if a graboid were to demonstrate a tracking ability related to vision, we would say that breaks the rules.

<u>Rule:</u> you can't see without eyes.

Supernatural entities play by their own set of rules even though they are not from our realm of existence. For an example, take a look at *Poltergeist*. It seems as if anything goes, the powers the titular poltergeist demonstrates range from: stacking chairs, causing visions, animating evil clown toys, taking control of trees, abducting little girls … you freakin' name it and it seems like it does it. "So," you might be asking, "what are its rules?"

Looking at the film, you might be able to guess it: the poltergeist is limited in its ability to interact with our plane of existence on a geographical level; the entity's origin is connected to the house having been built over a cemetary. (Interestingly, many people say the house was built on an Indian burial ground. However this doesn't come from the film but rather its sequel, *Poltergeist II: The Other Side* (1986), in which the filmmakers expanded on the lore to answer the question: why was the ghost only affecting this one household despite the entire subdivision resting on the cemetery.

The Shining is another film that blurs the rules of the ghosts' power. The question of their existence is as hard to answer as anything else in this cryptic film, though we will approach it as a supernatural film with psychological elements rather than a psychological film using supernatural elements—to simplify, for our discussion, the ghosts are real and not just within Jack Torrance's mind. Within the film, we know that young Danny Torrance has a kind of telepathy (a subject we will discuss later, along with magick) and so he is an easy target for the ghosts of the Overlook Hotel.

However, they also affect Jack and while the viewer might assume that Jack passed his gift—the shining—onto his son, it's never discussed or hinted at. The more immediate reading is to see Jack's weakness, his desire for a drink and the troubles in his family life, as leaving him susceptible to the malevolent influence of the ghosts. This reading is validated by the fact that all of the direct, physical violence in the film is located through the character of Jack.

However, we begin to enter a tricky area as the film progresses. Having knocked Jack out and locked him in a walk-in freezer, Wendy and Danny should be safe. At least, they should be if the ghosts are only able to interact with the physical plane through a human character that has been corrupted like Jack. But it is the ghosts themselves that let Jack out of the freezer, thus showing that they are capable of interacting with the physical world and provoking the question of why they need a human vessel in the first place. Earlier, Wendy suspects Jack of having abused Danny when he shows bruises and signs of physical assault. A psychological reading would place Jack as the culprit but with what we know from the later freezer interaction, the ghosts are indeed capable of physical assault.

And let's not even get into the photograph that closes out the film.

So, here again we have some confusing rules: just what can and can't these supernatural beings do? We know that they are confined to the Overlook, so we know that they have the same geographical rule as we saw in *Poltergeist*. But what they can do within that space is up in the air … or is it? Perhaps we are looking at these supernatural entities with the wrong lens. By exploring them as ghosts, we end up with confusion.

But what if they were less ghosts and more a spiritual embodiment of the corruptor trope? The corruptor is a character whose primary goal is to corrupt the protagonist, that is, to turn the protagonist evil or to show wickedness in the hearts of every man. The most famous example of the corruptor is, of course, Lucifer, the devil himself. I am not suggesting that the Overlook is hell or that Lloyd the bartender is Satan. Rather, he functions as a corruptor for an unknown reason and Jack signs his "deal with the devil" by accepting his drink despite his sobriety.

If the goal of the supernatural within the Overlook is not the deaths of Danny and Wendy but rather the corruption of Jack, then their actions begin to make sense. They attack Danny, not to hurt or kill him but to inject strife into Jack and Wendy's relationship. They let Jack out of the freezer not because he is the only one that could kill his family but because their deaths are only important if they are at his hands because of what the action represents if it comes from him.

The Shining appears not to have rules but that is due to its refusal to conform to the most readily known "laws" of the supernatural, instead borrowing elements of biblical significance (without conforming to a direct biblical metaphor).

For an example of a film that doesn't "play by the rules" as it were, let's examine *The Bye Bye Man* (2017). The basic premise is that there is a supernatural entity—the titular Bye Bye Man—that will come and kill you if you are aware of him. If you say his name, if you think his name, he comes closer and closer and anyone that you tell is now also infected with the curse. It's similar to *It Follows* in that it can be read as a metaphor for a transmittable disease. Unlike *It Follows*, in which you must sleep with someone to pass the curse along, *The Bye Bye Man* could be solved quite easily: don't tell anyone; it's a chain letter like those emails you use to get, if you don't pass it on then it dies with you.

Of course, the screenwriters must have realized this glaring plot hole and so they tried to work around it: the Bye Bye Man at one point touches the forehead of the lead character and that makes him start to have … tourettes? He struggles against saying "the Bye Bye Man" and comically clamps his hands to his mouth. If the Bye Bye Man can just make you say his name, then why doesn't he just do that? If the character from the 1960s doesn't want the curse to spread and has written "don't say it; don't think it" over and over again, then why would he write the name "Bye Bye Man" right after that?

Alright, so the rules of this universe are quite confusing and there is no concrete answer as to any of the questions it sparks. To make it even more confusing, though taking a step away from the supernatural rules themselves, our characters are told that the *only* way to deal with the situation is to "shoot the ones you told first and then kill yourself." But … ummm … the Bye Bye Man is coming to kill you so what exactly is this solving? I guess it's not to spread it anymore but we've already talked about how he can just make you say it, so what's the point? This is a film that wants to include many "spooky" moments but does so at the expense of a good story. Hell, there's even a scene that implies the Bye Bye Man prevented two of our characters from getting off … the hell are his powers again?

When dealing with the supernatural, the rules are paramount. Don't be a *The Bye Bye Man*; people might watch the film when it first comes out but it will fade away as quickly as it appeared. But enough about ghosts, ghouls, polter-spooks, and Bye Bye men, let's take a look at the supernatural we label as magick or psychic phenomena. From *The Lords of Salem* (2012) to *Scanners* (1981) and from *Carrie* (1976) to *The Craft* (1996), horror has invested a significant amount of time to the supernatural that we call **Parapsychology** (a word that lends a pseudo-scientific weight to telepathy, precognition, clairvoyance, psychokinesis and a whole world of entertaining gobbly gook).

Let's start with magick, that elusive beast. There are two key kinds, magic and magick. Magic is sawing people in half, pulling rabbits out of hats, and card tricks. Magick, on the other hand, is manipulating the forces and energies of the world through willpower and ritual. Some films, such as *Night of the Eagle* (1962) and *The Craft*, put a strong focus on these rituals—though, they are never fully explained but rather spoken about in a language that conveys the idea of the magick. For example, *The Craft* brings the idea of a "binding spell" into the movie in order to restrain a power hungry witch's magickal ability—we are told that is what the spell does, though we are asked to take it on faith that it will work for ... reasons?

The power behind the power, as it were, is never explained except for us to understand that there is a force out there that the magick user can tap into. It appears to be ruleless but in actuality it is governed by a set of rules that are inferred rather than explicit: power is linked to ritual, willpower, and desire; spells have to be cast and these have various degrees of success and various rituals required. But as the film moves towards the third act, the rules fade into the background. Characters start to exhibit powers because of the willpower they gain through their struggles—in following this route, which many magick focused films do, the power is related to character development rather than the magick as earlier ritualized. This is something that we will see shared with parapsychology films in a moment.

The Craft is unique—though not without its comrades—in having our main character be one of the magick users. A magick user may be one of our heroes, such as in *Night of the Eagle* and *The Devil Rides Out* (1968), though they are usually not our main character. This allows the filmmakers to educate the audience on magick by educating the protagonist to this newfangled world of the occult and it makes the laying out of rules that much simpler for the Scream Writer. Often, the character—and by extension us the viewer—don't need to know the intricate details of why a ritual requires what and how, so as long as we know not to break the protective salt barrier or to look a demon in the eyes or what other permutation of ritual we are presented (and the consequences if we do), then the audience will consider itself sufficiently informed.

The most common form of magick user in the horror film is the magick user as antagonist. Some films, such as *Rosemary's Baby* and *The House of the Devil*, use magick users whose occult practices are never shown to have any direct power in the way that the ladies of *The Craft* are. These films approach magick as a much more subtle practice: Minnie uses herbs and, supposedly, potions as the extent of her magickal power; while the Ulmans of *The House of the Devil* are shown having performed a ritual of some sort on the main character Samantha—the only sign of a direct, in the moment, manifestation of magick from the ritual is the splitting pain in Samantha's head and the horrific images that flash through her mind. These films tend to focus on atmosphere, paranoia, and tension—it is not about jump scares or wicked witches so much as it's about a feeling of helplessness in the face of the unknown.

Then there are those witches and warlocks that demonstrate magick with a direct impact in the here and now. *The Lords of Salem* shows the drug-like traces that malevolent magick forces onto the protagonist. Like *Leák* (*Mystics of Bali*, 1981) the character in *The Lords of Salem* doesn't appear to remember her nightly journeys through acid-washed occultism but the effect it is having on her life and state of mind is apparent throughout. *The Craft* gives us an evil witch in the form of Nancy, there's the warlock in *Warlock* (1989), and the witch in *The Witch*, and even the ghost of a witch in *The Conjuring*. These characters each have rules that they must follow:

Nancy and the warlock are beholden to rituals (except for when the film doesn't need them to be, a lazy writing habit that I beg you not to resort to); *The Witch* takes for its rules the mythology of witchcraft that was contemporary for the historical period; and *The Conjuring* ignores the witchcraft element and keeps it simple by focusing on the ghost aspect.

With each of these films taking a different approach to magick, there's not any one universal rule that Scream Writers should be following. Rather, what is important is to make sure that you set your own rules and that—regardless if you tell the audience the rules or not—you make sure that you never break them. We might not know the rules but audiences can tell when they are broken—we pick up on contradictions, they come across feeling wrong and will pull us out of the movie.

Finally, let's look at the parapsychological. *Carrie* is the story of an awkward young girl with telekinetic powers. The film, like so many good horror movies, is primarily about her story, which stands apart from the horror elements. Abusive religious mother, bullied at school, and finally coming into her own; it's an ugly duckling tale and we get caught up in it, hoping for the best for Carrie White. However, much like the journey of our protagonist in *The Craft*, this is a story about character growth and that growth is demonstrated through her powers.

When Carrie is pushed passed her breaking point, she snaps and in a fit of rage uses her powers to murder everyone at the local prom. We see a Cinderella story but once the clock strikes midnight there isn't a third act reunion with happiness. The element of the supernatural is the telekinetic powers and they are never explained—nor, do they have to be. We understand. She can move things with her mind and this happens most often when she is upset.

We understand this within ten minutes of the movie by seeing Carrie using them; we also understand that her use is subconscious, she doesn't know how she is doing what she does at first. Carrie comes, in time, to understand her powers but that understanding is a reflection of her growth towards a fully realized and independent person—her control of them demonstrates the willpower she as a character is learning to foster.

The *Final Destination* (2000–2011) movies are predicated on visions of horrific accidents in the future and how a character with the gift of precognition is able to save a handful of people because of their power. That is, they are able to save them from the first accident but then must use their powers to try to prevent death from claiming the would-be victims based on some design. The films posit two key supernatural elements: that death has a plan and will come after you if you avoid it, and that precognition exists. Apart from precognition, which the characters have to learn to deal with, these films are straightforward slasher movies.

Instead of a guy in a mask, the slasher is death itself and it wants to kill you in elaborate accidents. The precognition becomes an unwanted power of the protagonist, each time with a character that has never experienced anything like it before in their life. Being that the power is so new to them, they have to learn how to use it and make sense of it and so figuring out the rules of the power is a journey of discovery that the audience takes with the character.

Whether it's ghosts, witches, or telepathic precogs with telekinetic powers, the supernatural allows the Scream Writer to explore very interesting and diverse stories as long as they are able to lock down the rules. Because the supernatural is that which is not natural, these rules are what keep a story grounded and give the audience a frame of reference. In contrast, a monster movie does not have rules but rather biology, a set of rules we can understand because it follows (for the most part) the rules of the world we live in.

Possession, Ghosts, and Repressed Desires

In Kimberly Jackson's *Gender and the Nuclear Family in Twenty-First-Century Horror*, Jackson explores the *Insidious* films in terms of their representations of, unsurprisingly, gender in the family. However, Jackson hits an important point that highlights one of the reasons that possession is so terrifying within film. The act of possession often brings unspoken, repressed desires of the possessed person to the surface for all to see. For an example, let's use Jackson's own: *Poltergeist II: The Other Side*.

Jackson writes, "the focus is on the father's feelings of weakness. The father even briefly becomes 'possessed' and abuses his wife" (96). The feelings of weakness the father has violently express themselves through his possession, thus allowing the father to both work out his abusive rage and keep the role of acceptance partner and parental figure. This duality allows the father to be both abusive and loving, playing out his inner, repressed, fantasies under the protective coat of "I wasn't myself."

However, possession is not the only supernatural way for a character's repressed desires to be brought to the surface. Jackson uses *Poltergeist II* to contrast *Insidious*, the prime focus of her discussion in this particular chapter. Looking at the first *Insidious*, before the husband of Josh is possessed at the end, we see a series of ghosts that assault the family—particularly, they seem most interested in attacking Renai, the wife.

Jackson explores the way that the first ghost, the man that is seen pacing back and forth outside the Renai's window (only to suddenly appear inside and lunge at her), serves as a manifestation of "Josh's repressed rage"; the next ghost, being the bride in black that is actually a man in drag that hates his mother, suggests "there is some link between the man-bride's hatred for his mother and Josh's relationship to the women in his life" (87). In this way, Jackson is suggesting we pay attention to how the actions of the ghosts reflect the desires of Josh (who struggles with his image of self-worth because he doesn't make enough money, especially considering the hinted at midlife crisis that sees his wife staying home to work on her music).

When it comes to possession and haunting, the root cause often finds itself related to a perceived weakness within the human victim. Reagan played with a ouija board; Josh let stress and resentment eat away at him; Deborah Logan and the elderly patients of *The Exorcist III: Legion* (1990) suffer from Alzheimer's or dementia; Mia of *Evil Dead* (2013) is going through heroin withdrawls—our characters are often suffering, with this suffering being the weakness that allows evil to enter into their lives or even just into themselves. We identify the weakness as what lets the spirits in but it's easy to miss the fact that often these spirits are doing more than just terrorizing a victim: they are giving them what they secretly want.

In this way, ghosts and possessions are able to further the idea that a monster is rather just a monster: a haunting is rarely just a haunting but a way to explore the deeper desires, repressions and psychologies of the characters under assault.

<u>Weaknesses</u>

I know what you're thinking: "there's no way that *my* monster is weak, my monster is a deadly killing machine and there's no way to stop it." I don't want you to think I don't have anything but the utmost respect for your triple-armed-snake-monster but if you want the audience to enjoy the movie, you're gonna have to give it some kind of weakness (or, at the very least, the appearance of one). All movies are dependent on conflict and this is doubly so in horror movies; movies also require (or should require) a protagonist that pushes the plot forward with their actions.

When it comes to monster movies, this means that our protagonist is able to come up with a plan to fight back. Nine times out of ten, the monster is more physically threatening and powerful than the puny humans—so our characters will be forced to use human ingenuity and wit to escape the situation alive. Sometimes, this means the weakness of the monster is not a physical weakness but an inability to follow after a character. For example, in *Night of the Demons* (1988), the titular demons are confined to Hull House and the night of Halloween. This means that if our characters can survive through the night the demons will lose their power and our heroes will be able to escape from the property. The demons have a weakness, one that our characters exploit in their attempt to survive the film—some do, some don't, but there is a goal, an out, a plan, a weakness.

Let's say you sit down to watch a zombie movie or a vampire movie. These monsters come with culturally known weakness. Zombies—destroy the brain, burn the body. Vampires—sunlight, garlic, stakes to the heart, crosses, holy water, etc. It is these weaknesses that give characters a chance to fight back and possibly win.

Yes, the creatures are deadly but they are not unstoppable. When dealing with monsters that have entered into our pop culture lexicon such as these, the ability to subvert the expectations regarding their weaknesses arises. *Return of the Living Dead* has zombies that talk and zombies that just can't seem to die no matter what the hell happens to them. Because the writers knew the expected weaknesses, they were able to subvert that and make them into unstoppable monsters.

As an audience, we are shocked when they refuse to die and this emotional reaction fuels our enjoyment of the film. However, when a monster that's never been seen before just won't stop, we're often annoyed because there's no way for us as audience members to try to formulate a plan to escape it. Because the zombies in *Return of the Living Dead* seem to just be zombies, those creatures that have become mindless fodder in our video games, we think that we know how to stop them.

They reveal themselves to have no weakness but before this reveal they *appear* to have a weakness and this lets us engage with the situation of the film on a deeper level. Likewise, we now talk about Jason Voorhees as an unstoppable killing machine but this is only because he has returned for sequel after sequel; the end of every *Friday the 13th* movie has our protagonists stopping Jason—he has weaknesses, but they are then discarded so the next film can happen. In this way, Jason Voorhees is no different from Universal's Frankenstein—burned alive at the end of the first film?

No worries, he's back in the second. Explosion takes him out in the second? Well, he seems to be in pretty good shape when he's brought back in *Son of Frankenstein* (1939). Despite seemingly having no weakness, these films are always focused on a way of stopping the monster—otherwise, what the hell would there be for our characters to do? Just run and scream? That gets boring real quick, don't it?

There are many different ways to build weakness into your monsters without taking away their power. One of my favorite movie monsters of all time is Freddy Krueger. Freddy is a perfect example of our discussion on rules, as well: he can get you in your dreams. There we go, we have established the rules of the monster. We see Nancy pull his hat out of the dream world and this is why she is able to come up with a plan: You will wake me up while I'm holding Freddy so that we can beat him to death with baseball bats in the real world. It ain't fancy but it's something, it's a goal, it's exploiting a weakness.

This plan fails, however, and it is up to Nancy to figure out another way to beat him. Being that Krueger represents the boogeyman, that figure of childish fears, Nancy is able to take back her fear from him and thus drain him of his powers. This ties Freddy's weakness, based on the idea of what he represents, into Nancy's character arc and creates a powerful ending. Of course, this was all thrown out the window in the final scene—it turns out it's still a dream and nothing that just happened mattered. Wes Craven didn't want this ending but put it in at the studio's request so that there could be a sequel.

Krueger's weakness is one that is grounded within mythology: the boogeyman feeds on fear. Another example of weakness grounded within mythology is in *Leprechaun* (1993). In the first film, our titular Leprechaun is waylaid by having to shine shoes and his ultimate weakness is a four leaf clover. By tying the weaknesses of the Leprechaun into folklore and mythology, the film offers the characters a way to fight back. The mythology changes slightly by the second film. Here, the Leprechaun's weakness is iron.

Why is it iron? Why has it changed? This is never made clear and can be chalked up to how quickly the film was slapped together. However, it still gives our characters a way to fight back, like when one of them traps the Leprechaun in an iron safe; this scene is the highlight of the series, as it shows our Leprechaun now using his wits to prey on the characters weaknesses (his greedy nature) in order to escape his predicament. Our monsters might have weaknesses, but so do well written characters.

The most common form of weakness is a physical weakness. Take a look at *Jack Frost* (1997). It's a movie about a killer mutant snowman, so heat and antifreeze become the primary ways of stopping him. The dolls in *Dolls* are tiny little porcelain figures, their weakness is the size and strength of the humans but they attack in swarms and overwhelm the characters. And what about our trusty ol' graboids? Well, they can't see and hunt off of sound. Our characters use this to trick them into eating dynamite.

When that doesn't work, they are forced to come up with another solution: if they hunt by sound, then someone (if they have the guts) can trick them into going off a cliff. They can't see it coming, they have to get up to top speed to chase after our character, so they have no way of slowing down to avoid the fall. Our characters are forced to assess the situation and come up with a plan in order to get out of it and that plan depends on the monster's weakness.

So take a look at your triple-armed-snake-monster. If you were stuck in the situation with it, how would you try to get out? What elements of your monsters can you twist to your advantage? Are the monsters based on magic? Can you attack the source of the magic to kill the monster? Does it have a mythology that our characters can exploit? Is there a Necronomicon they can burn? If there's no way for our characters to survive, then why are we watching? Who just wants to watch pointless death? Sure, maybe most or all of them do die but at least give them a fighting chance first.

Staging the Big Reveal

Now that we have explored the creation of the monster within our story, it's time to talk about how we show our monsters. The last thing that we want to do is provide room for what Rich Evans of Red Letter Media calls the "Coupon Shot"—a reveal that has no tension or escalation, a shot that feels as if the filmmakers just said "here ya go!" (For a perfect example of the "Coupon Shot," take a look at *Best of the Worst: Episode 50* and the discussion of 1985's *Biohazard*. It'll be less painful than watching the movie.) So let's take a look at a few examples of some great monster reveals and how they were accomplished.

The Thing is a masterpiece of practical effects and everyone remembers the spider-head and the defibrillator death. But before we get to all of the craziness of the titular Thing and see its many forms (we'll talk about utilizing the many reveals of an evolving monster in a bit), we are first introduced to the grotesque body horror of our space monster in the dog kennel. Let's take a look at how Bill Lancaster's screenplay handles this feat. First, the dog enters the kennel and "remains a statue." While the other dogs growl, hiss, and bark, our Dog-Thing does nothing until … suddenly, a scene heading brings our attention to "THE SHADOW OF THE DOG" followed by the description telling us that "The shadow suddenly lurches upward, seeming larger."

We're never given a good view of what exactly our Dog-Thing looks like. When our characters get there, the light has already been broken—here, screenwriter Bill Lancaster is controlling the choices of the electrical department and preventing his monster from being over lit (which is one of the quickest ways to have your effect's "strings be shown"). It also prevents our characters from having a good view of the creature, now having to rely on flashlights which only illuminate the creature in bits and pieces—"some 'thing'. A dog. But not quite. Impossible to tell." Later, we're shown "a large, bristly, arachnid-like leg."

And guess what? That's all we see.

We hear the noises it makes but we are lost in the confusion of the situation along with the characters. Not only does this preserve the mystery of what we are seeing and dealing with (how can a dog have an arachnid-like leg?) but it also helps to ground us within the emotional situation of the characters—our experience is just as chaotic as theirs and despite having the privileged position of audience members (or readers), we are just as lost and confused. And what's more … scared. What we are seeing defies what we know about the world (that dogs are dogs and arachnids are arachnids). By controlling the information we are given, Lancaster leaves the audience asking questions and at a loss to understanding the situation. In time, the characters and us will learn what we're dealing with and the characters will be able to come up with a plan to exploit the creature's weakness. But in this first reveal, there is nothing but terror, confusion … nothing but some …"thing."

Let's take a look at one more film, Ridley Scott's *Alien* (1979). *Alien* is a film with not just one great monster reveal but four of them. Three of these reveals demonstrate different stages within the xenomorph (though in the film it is simply called the alien). The first of these reveals happens when the crew members of the spaceship *Nostromo* explore the moon LV-426 in response to a distress call. They find that the distress signal comes from a derelict alien ship.

Inside the ship they find the remains of a large alien species that's chest seems to have burst open from the inside out. Moving deeper into the ship, crewmember Kane finds a chamber filled with hundreds upon hundreds of eggs. Kane examines one of the eggs which causes it to burst open, and "with shocking violence, a small creature smashes outward." The language of the screenplay by Walter Hill and David Giler lets us know the speed at which this happens. Thus, the director knows that we only see a flash of the creature, it's a reveal within a jump scare, we're too shocked to fully take in the monster.

This first reveal happens so quickly because it's a rule of thumb that you don't want to give your monster away too early. So it might seem a mistake when Kane, with the creature—a "facehugger"—attached to his face, is brought onto the ship and is shown at length within the sickbay. But *Alien* knows exactly what it's doing because this crab-like creature is far from the alien's final form, as we learn with what might be the most famous monster reveal of all time: the "chestburster."

The facehugger has relinquished Kane, everything seems normal. The danger has passed. There is a lighthearted atmosphere as the crew of the *Nostromo* gather around the mess hall table. Small talk, jokes, smiles, laughter … all is fine. All seems well (a tactic to create powerful scares that we'll discuss in more depth next chapter) when out of nowhere Kane begins to choke and convulse. The danger has passed, the alien is dead, what the hell could be happening?

Then the moment that's impossible to forget: Kane's shirt bulges out in a spray of blood from his chest. The crew is shocked for a moment but regain their composure and try to help their friend when, suddenly, blood sprays across the room as Kane's ribs and chest split apart and a little parasitic worm-like creature with razor sharp teeth bursts forth in a fountain of gore. It has a moment to take in its surroundings before it dashes out of the room to find a hiding spot.

With this scene, *Alien* uses several tools to stage an absolutely pants-shitting reveal of the chestburster. First, the scene happens in a moment of peace; the passing of the threat means a lowering of the guard in the characters and when the characters lower their guard the audience usually does as well. This trick can be seen put to similar use in *Jaws* when Brody lays down a chum line: they are trying to attract the shark but they have no reason to suspect it has already found them and so the moment of calm is pierced by the sudden arrival (and is made even more shocking in the fact that Brody has his back turned to the monster, more on that in a moment). So with the audience lulled into a state of calm, they are shocked when that calm is broken.

But we don't immediately see the chestburster. Instead, the characters and the audience first think Kane is choking on his food. When it's made clear that there's something more going on, the crew lays Kane onto the table and treats his episode the way you would treat a seizure. A seizure is already a shocking event and, unlike space aliens and chestbursters, one that audience members can relate to the world they live in. The first half of this scene is able to shock the audience but even within that shock, the film is tricking them.

Then comes the blood.

A great spurt that arcs through the air and startles the characters and the audience. The focus had been on treating the seizure, making sure that Kane doesn't bite off his tongue, so we are focused not on his chest but on his head. We are left completely unprepared for this—not only because of the misdirected focus but also by the sheer inconceivability of it: bodies just don't do whatever Kane's just did! At this point, we still don't realize that we are in a monster reveal moment. Neither do the characters, and so they continue trying to help Kane in the only way they know how.

Moments later this first spurt of blood is followed by a geyser of blood as some object, some … thing, pushes a good foot out of Kane's chest with an animal screech. Now the film lingers on the creature, it lets the audience try to understand it in a lingering eight second shot. The screenplay suggests this lingering shot by spending four lines of description to paint the picture of a "disgusting little head" that is "trailing a thick, wormlike tail." Once again, lingering on our alien for this much time serves to diminish the chestburster's power for subsequent scares. But remember, we're in the hands of talented Scream Writers and they're already a step ahead of the audience.

So there's a parasitic worm alien running around on the ship and our crew is going to have to kill it before they go back into cryosleep, otherwise they're as helpless as a tv dinner. The crew moves together, using a motion tracker, as they work their way through the ship in an attempt to catch it (they can't just kill it, its acid blood would eat through the hull of the ship) and throw it out the airlock. Thinking they're right on top of the alien, they are startled when the ship's cat jumps out and goes scurrying away. One of the crew members, Brett, is sent to catch the cat so that it doesn't set off the motion tracker again.

As Brett is trying to coax the kitty out of its hiding spot, the alien sneaks behind him and kills him. The screenplay has this to say: "The Alien. Now seven feet tall. Hanging from the undercarriage strut in reverse position." That's all we see of it in the screenplay. Despite screaming and drawing the attention of his crew mates, when pressed on what they saw they can only say, "Whatever it was, it was big. Swung down on him like a giant fucking bat."

So we know that the alien has grown but that's all we are able to tell from this. Like the shark in *Jaws* it is revealed to be a) larger than we thought and b) places the character(s) in unknown danger. But unlike the facehugger and the chestburster steps in the xenomorph's evolution, we aren't given time to fully understand what we've seen.

The screenplay gives us only a single line of description (its height) and the film maintains this air of mystery by first placing the alien in the background of the shot and then focusing on super tight close-ups that only reveal singular features of the alien rather than show it as a whole. Because we aren't able to get a full image of the alien, our imaginations are able to take over and fill in the blanks with the most horrendous things imaginable.

Your creature might be terrifying but the depths of our minds are worse.

Finally, I would be remiss if I didn't mention the amazing reveal at the end of the movie. This is less a reveal of the monster itself and more a shock to the audience because they had thought it was dead. Ripley, the only survivor left from our crew, is in an escape pod and preparing herself to go into cryosleep for the long journey back to human occupied space. Everything is quiet, the movie is winding down, and we are finally able to breathe after the tension of the previous twenty minutes. Suddenly, the alien's arm drops out from between the power cables and electronics of the pod and startles Ripley and us. (Re-watching this scene to write this section, it still got me!).

The alien rolls over, it's taking a nap—after all, it's just a dumb animal and it's just eaten a whole crew worth of tasty humans. This reveal demonstrates one more terrifying way of showing your monster: hiding them in plain sight. The gleaming black exterior of the xenomorph blends in perfectly with the shadows and cables of the escape pod, we didn't even realize we were looking right at it until that arm falls into view. This is used for an effective jump scare in this scene but it is put to further use in *Aliens* (1987) when we start to realize that the walls of the complex our space marine characters are in are swarming with xenomorphs—their natural camouflage keeping them hidden from view.

This is a tactic that has been used in many films such as *Ghostwatch* (1992), *Insidious*, *The Descent*, *The Strangers* (2008), *Profondo Rosso* (*Deep Red* (1975), which uses it as a major plot point), *The Grudge 2* (2006), *Dead Silence* (2007), *Kairo* (*Pulse*, (2001)), *It Follows* ... there's a ton of them. These reveals can be handled two ways: either the character doesn't notice (and therefore the reveal doesn't bring attention to itself) or the character notices and it causes a scare (such as in *Alien*). Personally, I am a huge fan of hiding the monster in plain sight and not calling attention to it—let the audience find it, have it terrify them on a rewatch.

Take a look at your screenplay. How do you reveal your monster? Have you shown them too much? Is it clear what they are immediately or do you keep it vague, in shadows, or only seen in flashes? What is happening when they are revealed? Are characters aware of them? How do the characters react? Ask yourself these questions and explore the different techniques above, perhaps it would be a stronger reveal if your triple-armed-snake-monster was shown behind your character rather than in front. What if we only see the tail? What will we think the monster is then? Remember that you're writing what the audience is supposed to see—show them too much and you won't affect them the way you want to.

<u>Description</u>

Let's have a brief discussion about description to close out this chapter. This could easily be a large section or even a chapter on its own but I don't believe that's necessary. I have elected to focus on those elements that are unique to the horror screenplay rather than write yet another book that takes about the generals of form, structure, character, et. al. Those books exist, far too many of them in fact. But one of the key elements that they all share and that is no different in the horror screenplay is that brevity and concise language are important. This is a given of the medium, not the genre, and horror is no different.

When it comes to describing your monsters, decide what to focus on. Do you want to give a clear picture of what the monster looks like or do you want to convey the feeling of the monster? These questions are strikingly similar to what you should ask yourself when staging the reveal of your monster. However, the reveal focuses on the elements of revealing the monster within the story, description is the focus on the appearance of your monster. And there is no right answer here; unlike with describing character, where if you reveal clothing or race or hair color then it better have a purpose, what you choose to describe about your monster is up to you and what the monster needs to do. If it's a triple-armed-snake-monster, then it's pretty specific and you need to convey those specifics. If it's a werewolf, however, you can describe the essence of it—it is more wolf than human, a bestial force of destructive power that walks on its hind legs, for example. My favorite description of any monster in the history of screenwriting comes from James Cameron's screenplay for *The Terminator* (1984): "It looks like death rendered in steel." Cameron then spends an action line to hit the important details (such as the sounds it makes and its glowing red eyes) but within that single line we know everything we need to know about the terminator.

When editing a script, you cut it to the bone. Unnecessary description gets jettisoned. It doesn't matter if it's the description of the gothic castle the action takes place, or of your three-armed-snake-monster. Don't be afraid to over describe your monsters in the first draft. But don't hesitate when it comes to cutting back. Capture the essence and any specifics that truly matter in as concise a way as possible.

Exercises

1. If you have a monster in mind already, fill out as much information as you can about it: What does it eat? What temperatures does it like? Where does it nest? Is it nocturnal? Write down everything you can possibly think of. This will get you thinking about aspects of your monster you hadn't considered yet and could reveal patterns and ideas that were hidden before.

2. List as many descriptive words as you can about your monster—slimey, scaly, bestial, monstrous, furry, hairy, etc. Then go over your list, saying the words out loud in sentences about the monster, listen to how each word makes you feel, explore the connotations. Nothing is more disappointing than when our terrifying monsters come off as cute and cuddly because of a poorly chosen descriptive word.

3. Stepping back from the awesome brute force and abject visage of your monster, spend some time exploring how its origins and use in the story give thematic weight. What created the monster? What does its birth imply? What are its reasons for killing?

4. Take some time to think about how your monster interacts with the protagonist. Is it merely a monster for them to fight or does it hold a deeper significance? If your monster has no relationship to your protagonist, can this

be altered? If, for example, your character suffers from agoraphobia, then a monster in the basement forms a thematic connection to their psychology (the monster too doesn't leave the house, is it a personification of agoraphobia?). What does your monster say about the world of your character?

Chapter 3: Scares

I think crafting a new, effective horror movie is not just about when night falls and things get scary. It's about setting a tone and mood that permeates throughout the entire movie. So even during the daytime, things are never quite safe-feeling.

James Wan

The purpose of film—of any art, really—is to provoke a response within the viewer. While this response can be of an intellectual nature (such as *An Inconvenient Truth*'s (2016) goal of making its audience confront and think about global warming), art is most often after an emotional response. Melodramas gained the adjective "weepy" for their tendency to provoke sadness; action films are often called "thrilling" because their pace rarely lets up, action set pieces often move so quickly and contain so many twists and turns that the audience doesn't have time to digest what they're seeing. In her essay, *Her Body, Himself: Gender in the Slasher Film*, Carol J. Clover coined the term "body" genre.

The body genre, she suggests, is made up of those genres of films that seek to provoke a bodily sensation. Clover includes only horror and pornography within this label, though it was later extended by Linda Williams to include melodramas (and it seems a drastic oversight on

Clover's part to not have identified the comedy with this labeling). So the horror genre is one that, as a piece of art, tries to provoke an emotional reaction and, as a "body" genre, a physical reaction within the viewer.

In this chapter we will explore at length the many ways that the horror film has adopted to achieve this goal and how the Scream Writer can learn to make use of these strategies. From shock to disgust, suspense to atmosphere, tension to anxiety, there are many tools available for use in scaring the shit out of the audience (a term that directly links fear to abjection). But not every tool is equal and so it is important to understand the specific and emotional reaction that you are aiming to achieve. To explore the differences between these tools we will first examine their definitions in order to understand the cognitive effect they have and the interactions between the effects. From there we will explore each of these tools in depth, through examples from popular horror films, in order to understand how they have grown and evolved and we'll examine the many different approaches to these tools so we can understand the flexibility they offer.

Defining Our Fears, Apprehensions, and Anxieties

Let's begin our deep dive into the semantics of horror by starting with the word itself. Being that as Scream Writers we are working within the horror genre, it seems as good of a place to start as any. However, as our examination of the toolbox will demonstrate, the definitions of the various elements we work with have a tendency to fold back into each other. The effects we are aiming to achieve are so often related to each other, this shouldn't come as much of a surprise. This does eliminate a clear jumping off point for our discussion though. So while we will be looking at horror first, this conversation could just as easily start with shock, fear, suspense, et. al.

We covered the definition of horror when we explored the many ways the horror genre has been defined. Horror is "an intense feeling of fear, shock, or disgust." If we look at the horror genre as defined by its label, as opposed to the definitions provided by various scholars, then this definition enlightens us to two key points to keep in mind. First, the horror genre is more than just an attempt to provoke fear.

We know this because of the second point: horror is also composed of shock and disgust. This means that Torture Porn films that aren't scary but just disgusting are still achieving a form of horror (the effect as well as the genre). Personally, I am not a fan of this subgenre (I never made it past the second *Saw* movie) but it is doing a disservice to claim they fail as horror movies because of a lack of scares.

We know that horror is composed of fear, shock, or disgust, so we now know three of the tools we can call upon to help us horrify our audiences. Let's take these one at a time and see what we can learn from the definition of each. Starting with fear, we find its definition as a noun to mean "an unpleasant emotion caused by the belief that someone or something is dangerous, likely to cause pain, or a threat." When used as a verb it means "to be afraid of (someone or something) as likely dangerous, painful, or threatening." Further, let's take a look at the definition of terror while we are discussing fear because terror is defined as "extreme fear."

Fear as a noun (the emotion itself) or as a verb (the act of being within the emotion) both share three key points: danger, pain, and threat. We know that danger means "able or likely to cause harm or injury," and pain is "physical suffering or discomfort caused by illness or injury" (though as a verb it expands to include the realm of mental suffering, so we will append "physical or mental suffering" to our definition going forward). Finally, threat is defined as "a person or thing likely to cause damage or danger." Taking these definitions a step further, we can see that fear is primarily focused on pain; that is, danger and threat both cause fear because of the possibility of pain. Therefore, fear itself represents fear of pain.

But now we have a problem: the audience is not harmed by watching a movie, so how can we cause them fear? We will solve this paradox later in the chapter. For now, let's move onto shock. We find shock defined as "a sudden upsetting or surprising event or experience." To shock someone is to "cause (someone) to feel surprised and upset."

Surprise means unexpected, so shock is the cognitive effect of having been surprised by an upsetting event. As we will see, the most common form of shock used within the horror genre is the jump scare but there are also ways to shock the audience on an ideological, spiritual, intellectual, or fundamental level. Therefore, we should not think of shock simply as a sudden loud noise but keep in mind its definition that it is not just "sudden" but also "surprising" and "upsetting."

Finally, the last element that defines horror is disgust. Disgust is "a feeling of revulsion or profound disapproval aroused by something unpleasant or offensive." Interestingly, this definition expands what is typically thought of as disgusting within the horror genre. Revulsion (defined as "a sense of disgust or loathing") is a nice description of what I feel when I watch *August Underground's Mordum* (2003) because I find the actions depicted within to be loathsome ("causing hatred or disgust; repulsive"). We explored in the previous chapter the idea of the abject and how it serves to disgust and how a feeling of abjection can be caused on an ideological level. This is true of disgust also, as we see it defined as "unpleasant or offensive." This is how I can find your politics to be disgusting (because they offend me) or be disgusted by having to stay late at work (because it is unpleasant). This is also how my mother can find *Funny Games* (1997, 2007) to be an absolutely disgusting movie despite the fact that there is no gore and little blood.

Now we understand what is meant by horror and we have gained three powerful tools that we can use to provoke horror. But these three aren't the only tools at our disposal. Let's also quickly explore what we mean by suspense, tension, dread, unease, and atmosphere.

Suspense is "a state or feeling of excited or anxious uncertainty about what may happen." This definition is important for two reasons. We'll look at the second in a moment but the first is that suspense is created through uncertainty. While we're talking about suspense, let's also take a look at tension because it is "mental or emotional strain; intense suppressed suspense, anxiety, or excitement." Tension and suspense would seem to be intricately connected but we'll have to wait until we explore these tools in depth to understand their relationship better.

Dread is defined as "anticipate with great apprehension or fear." Apprehension is "anxiety or fear that something bad or unpleasant will happen." Therefore, dread is a magnification of apprehension and apprehension is a magnification of suspense. Finally, let's take a look at unease as it will highlight a key thread that has been running throughout our investigations.

Unease is simply "anxiety or discontent." Anxiety, "a feeling of worry, nervousness, or unease, typically about an imminent event or something with an uncertain outcome." Anxiety is included in the definitions of suspense, tension, apprehension (and therefore dread), and unease. We know, too, that fear arises from the belief that the thing or person we're afraid of is likely to cause harm and therefore we can see fear as an extension of anxiety.

The horror genre, more than showing a hideous monster or the rampage of a psychopathic mind, is about making the audience feel anxious. Disgust and shock do not focus on anxiety themselves but are tools that help to bring anxiety out of the audience by confronting them with unpleasant stimuli. However, the goal should not be purely to disgust or purely to shock but weave these reactions into a tapestry of anxieties.

With this understanding of the cognitive effects that our tools elicit, let's finish our lesson of semantics by exploring the atmosphere. Defined as "the pervading tone or mood of a place, situation, or work of art." Now of course, we are building works of art so that should stand out but it tells us nothing about how it is made. However, it does also mention place or situation and we will be exploring both of these in the near future. But first, let's break the atmosphere down a little further.

Tone is "the general character or attitude of a place, piece of writing, situation, etc." Character here does not refer to the personalities that populate our artworks but rather to the "main or essential nature" of the referent. Mood is defined as "inducing or suggestive of a particular feeling or state of mind." Atmosphere is then a combination of the essential nature and the feeling of a particular artwork.

By understanding how we manipulate the character and feeling of a work, we understand how we change its atmosphere. Atmosphere is more than just a tool that we can insert into our work (such as shock or disgust), it is the sum of every tool working in conjunction.

Horror: Making Use of Fear, Shock, and Disgust

In this section we will be looking at how to use the three key elements that make up horror: fear, shock, and disgust. Examining how movies have used these elements in the past will help us to understand the many ways that we are able to use them as we push forward as the Scream Writers of the future.

Fear

As we discovered when we broke down the definition of fear, it is an emotion that is focused on "the belief that someone or something is dangerous or likely to cause pain." This left us with the paradox: how can a clearly fictional artwork cause fear? Using fear itself is not so hard, *Halloween* provokes fear through the figure of Michael Myers, *A Nightmare on Elm Street* has Freddy Krueger, *The Last House on the Left* (1972) has the all too human Krug—these films are all examples of the use of a character that is "dangerous or likely to cause pain" and as such they work within the boundaries of fear. Of course, there are also phobias ("extreme or irrational" fears) and we can easily see how *Eight Legged Freaks* (2002) or the aptly named *Arachnophobia* would cause fear in audience members with arachnophobia. But it's also irrational to be afraid of two-dimension images projected on a screen. So how is it that fear is provoked in the rational viewer?

The key to unlocking this paradox is found within the writings of Samuel Taylor Coleridge, who, in 1817, coined the term "willing suspension of disbelief." Justifying his inclusion of supernatural elements in *Lyrical Ballads, with a Few Other Poems*, Coleridge wrote in *Biographia Literaria*: "that my endeavours should be directed to persons and characters supernatural ... so as to transfer from our inward nature a human interest and a semblance of truth sufficient to procure for these shadows of imagination that willing suspension of disbelief for the moment." This quote is not only noteworthy for having coined the phrase but also for identifying the key ingredient that we as Scream Writers require in order to make our audiences fear.

We need to cause a suspension of disbelief and to do so we need to ground ourselves within human interest and the semblance of truth. I do not devote a section of this book to discussing characters, this is because characters are an aspect shared across creative or screenwriting and not unique to the horror screenplay as such. However, Coleridge was able to identify in 1817 the importance of character to the suspension of disbelief.

We can only cause fear through this suspension, therefore in order to cause fear we must have characters that speak to our human interest (but this doesn't mean that we have to like them). We must have characters with a semblance of truth so that we can willingly suspend our disbelief (that we are merely watching actors at play) and belief that the characters we are seeing are real in every sense of the word. They have real emotions, mental processes, struggles, experiences … that they are alive. It is only through our characters that we can make an audience fear.

In my work as a screenplay consultant, I encounter scripts that are far from ready for being made into movies. The major issue within these scripts is not the writing itself (though, truthfully, that is often the biggest detriment in regards to getting agents or studios to read them) but within the choices of characters. In these screenplays, characters often make choices that go against the values they have established, demonstrate knowledge that they couldn't possibly have (unless they had a copy of the script, too), or are just not characters (they are the illusion of a character but lack that feeling of reality, they fall within the uncanny valley). If our characters aren't real, we can't expect the audience to fear for them.

Further, we can extend Coleridge's quote beyond the realm of the character. Character is the first and most important thing to give a semblance of truth but this has to also carry forward into our threats themselves. Freddy Krueger, Michael Myers, the ghosts of *The Conjuring* and *The Conjuring 2* (2016), all of these threats must give the semblance of truth. However, truth does not mean reality because we are playing with the supernatural here (not true of the first *Halloween* which we will discuss momentarily).

The audience of horror is willing to suspend their disbelief and accept the supernatural elements of our stories as existing within the reality of the stories; however, as we discussed in the previous chapter, the rules of the supernatural have to make sense or, if not exactly sense then, not contradict themselves. The reality of our surreal aspects must be able to exist within the world we have placed ourselves into, the world of the characters. As characters are often human, we see them as reflecting the rules of the reality that we live in; the supernatural reflects the rules of the reality we are allowing ourselves to believe in, therefore it is of utmost importance that this fictionalized reality appears to be real in its own right.

When our threats are not supernatural, such as in *Halloween* or *Henry: Portrait of a Serial Killer*, we again see the importance of character first in establishing fear. The threats in these worlds are human threats and therefore must be given a human dimension. That is not to say that *Halloween* needs a scene where we see Michael Myers' going about his day, cooking himself a nice meal, connecting with a stranger on the street—the human aspect of Michael comes from his adherence to the rules of physics and biology (at least until the very last moment and the sequels). Myers' reacts when bodily trauma is inflicted on him, he is shown to require food when Dr. Loomis and Sheriff Brackett find the remains of a dog he had partially eaten.

Because Michael is a man, and governed by human reality, the scene that most gets called out as a mistake or a plot hole comes at the beginning of the film. Michael is locked up in a mental asylum for killing his sister when he was six. The film then jumps fifteen years later to the night that Michael escapes from the mental hospital. His method of escape? He steals a car and drives off. However, Michael has been locked up for those fifteen years and therefore shouldn't know how to drive a car. Because of the strong filmmaking and characters, *Halloween* is not dragged down by this fracture in it's semblance of truth.

We can't all make *Halloween*, however.

The Scream Writer is the first line of defence in the battle of ensuring suspension of disbelief.

Fear is the emotion that arises from "the belief that someone or something is dangerous, likely to cause pain, or a threat." In order for the audience to believe that something within the fictional world is a threat, they have to willingly suspend their disbelief. However, a suspension of disbelief does not mean that the audience believes themselves to be in danger (though this has been done successfully in rare cases such as *Ghostwatch*) but that they believe the characters are in danger. The only way a character can be in danger is for the audience to believe in the character and the world in which the character exists. When successful, we believe that these characters are in harm's way and this causes us to be afraid.

But there is another kind of fear, one that doesn't require us to believe the characters are in danger. There is the fear that arises from psychological horror or from witnessing a character's descent into madness. There is a fear that arises within us when we are confronted with the reality that is insanity or psychopathy; this is a fear that arises from the idea that "it could happen to you." This is an intellectual fear, a fear that arises in the mind of the audience, rather than plays out across the screen. It arises out of a confrontation of our expectations about, and our views of, the world. Intellectual fear builds with reflection after the fact. In this way, intellectual fear is about a danger to the self, the audience rather than the characters, and shares a lot with the power of fundamental shocks.

Shock

With shock we are dealing not with an emotion itself but with events that "cause someone to feel surprised and upset." This means that to harness the power of shock, we have to build shocking moments and events into our screenplays. The most obvious, and overused, form of shock in the horror genre is the jump scare—that sudden loud noise that assaults the senses and causes your ass to leap out of the seat. Though it is far from being the only form of shock that Scream Writers can leverage, because it is the most common we will begin with it and then move onto the less common (though, I will argue, more effective) forms of shock such as ideological shocks.

Jump Scares

A jump scare is caused by a sudden change within the scene and almost always relies on a spike in the audio volume. This serves to surprise the audience, to jostle them out of the state of calm or anxiousness that you have put them in. Because jump scares rely on the unexpected, to truly be effective it's important that the audience doesn't see them coming. This may seem counter to some of the movies to have come out in recent years, such as the *Paranormal Activity* series.

Watching the third film of the series with an audience in the theatre was an interesting, though confusing, experience. In these films, we are mostly watching nothing; that is, because these are found footage films that want to give the illusion of reality, they focus on non-events and the day-to-day activities of the characters. However, from time to time, the film primes us to expect a ghostly encounter and delivers a jump scare.

Crowd watching, I found the audience to be chatting and generally not paying attention to the boring bits of the movies—as these are so story lite, this maybe doesn't come as a surprise but it's an odd behaviour within a twenty-first century theatre. However, when the "scary" bits approached, the audience quieted down and tensed up. This lasted until the jump scare, at which point there were screams and laughs. Then everyone went back to what they were doing.

It was clear that the film was delivering a shock but beyond that, the audience wasn't taking away anything of substance from the film. Contrast that with *The Conjuring* or *Insidious*. Both of these films have absolutely pants shitting jump scares, but they also deliver a story that invests the audience and uses techniques of tension and suspense to keep the audience on the edge of their seat throughout, rather than just when the film announces "the spooky bit is coming!"

A well executed jump scare feeds off of the suspense and tension of a film—the more tense the moment, the more powerful the shock. Suspense can leave the audience unnerved and that straining of their nerves leaves them "victim" to the jump scare. Because we'll see how to build tension and suspense in a little while, we won't be covering them in depth here, though we will be discussing them as we examine some historic jump scares. But first, let's talk about what NOT to do when it comes to a jump scare (or, because I don't believe in one-for-one rules, at least understand why you are doing them and how you can use them in new ways):

1. <u>Fake Out Scare</u>—this is a jump scare caused by something completely innocuous. Sometimes the fake-out is used to set up the real thing, the idea being that releasing the tension through something innocent leaves the audience unprepared for the real scare that follows it.

Due to the over use of this device, it comes off as disingenuous and cheap unless it is handled with the utmost care.

2.   Spring-Loaded Cat—this is a fake out scare of the worst kind. Our characters hear a noise, they investigate, it seems to be coming from the closest. They prepare themselves for the worst and slowly open it … and holy shit, someone threw a cat at me! The problem with the spring loaded cat is that it is a fake out scare that almost always lacks reason and comes across as absolute bullshit. It worked in *Alien*, but you'll be hard pressed to find another scene that effective. The spring-loaded cat has also been used to set up a real jump scare, but even this has been done to death as evidenced from the episode of *Community* (2009-2015) where cats just keep jumping out of nowhere.

3.   The Mirror Scare—I'm brushing my teeth, just gonna duck my head to spit … I'm opening up the medicine cabinet, got my pills, time to close it and … WHOA, SCARY FACE! This is a jump scare that goes back at least to 1965's *Repulsion*, and it hasn't felt fresh in years. Audiences are so prepared for a mirror jump scare (the same way they are prepared for a scene in a car to have a crash) that setting up a mirror scene that doesn't have a jump scare is an easy way to make your audience anxious (relying solely on their pop cultural knowledge)

Some people see *The Phantom of the Opera* (1925) as the first jump scare. The phantom is unmasked to reveal his hideous visage. This reveal is definitely one of cinema's earliest shocks but it plays more on disgust and abjection than what we think of now as a jump scare. I would place the first jump scare proper as the "Lewton Bus" in *Cat People*. While this moment is a fake out scare, it didn't have the 100+ years of film history we have now to inform it.

In *Cat People,* Oliver Reed marries Irena Dubrovna. Irena hails from Serbia and is convinced she is cursed by an old legend of her people that says she will turn into a fierce cat in the heat of passion. Because of this fear, Irena and Oliver are never able to get physically close and this begins to drive a wedge into their relationship. Oliver shares his troubles with Alice Moore, a co-worker that he is close friends with.

One night Oliver stays late at work and joins Alice for a coffee and discusses the problems he's facing at home. Neither of them realize that Irena has followed them to the cafe and has been watching over their conversation, her jealousy going through the roof. Oliver thanks Alice for listening and they both leave their separate ways to head home. Alice walks down a lonely street, the sidewalk flanked by a stone wall, the street lights offering only patches of illumination that give way to deep shadows.

Irena follows after her, her footsteps clanking against the cobblestones and echoing through the quiet night. We cut from Alice's feet to Irenas, then to a medium shot of Alice walking through the glow of a street light. Irena should be right behind her, we hear her footsteps speed up but she never shows and then … silence. A moment passes before Alice begins to slow, aware that the footsteps are gone and finding the silence unnerving.

She looks over her shoulder, there is just an empty street. She begins to run, something isn't right but she doesn't know what. There are no paths for a stranger to step off to, it's as if the steps previously were from a ghost. She clutches a light post, looking over her shoulder as the growl of a large cat can be heard. This is it for her! But then no, a bus finishes pulling up and the sound joins its engine and the opening of its door, she's saved. Only now, as she steps onto the bus does she notice the swaying of the bushes above the stone wall and how they slowly come to rest as if someone, or something, has quickly departed from behind them.

The "Lewton Bus" of *Cat People* might not make a whole lot of sense if we think too hard about it: How was it she never noticed it coming? Where were its headlights to light up the night? It's a fake out scare and one that fails at logic. But as an example of how to pull off a killer jump scare? It can't be beat. Let's take a look at why it's so effective.

First, the audience is tense. We know that Irena is following her, though Alice doesn't. This is a case of **Dramatic Irony**: the audience knows what the character(s) do not. As the scene begins, we are on edge because we expect something bad to happen: Will Irena turn into a large cat and kill Alice? Will they end up in a verbal or physical confrontation over Irena's jealousy of Alice's role in her husband's life? We have an

Expectation (that something bad will happen) and this guides us through the scene.

Second, Alice becomes worried after the footsteps stop. We the audience are still in on the dramatic irony of the scene except that when Alice turns around we realise that we don't know where Irena is anymore. We have an understanding of the situation that Alice has failed to grasp but we are also now thrown into the same unknowing of Alice because we no longer have the spatial knowledge we did before (that Irena was behind Alice).

Instead, we know that Irena is angry at Alice but not where she is and, though we have our expectations, what she will do. We have gone from a place of knowledge with an expectation to a place of **Unknowing** with an expectation. Our guards rise—no longer are we tense about what will happen when Irena confronts Alice, we are now tense about what will happen to us (will we be surprised, scared, annoyed, etc?) when the confrontation happens.

Third, Alice continues to throw glances behind her and we see the empty street. Combined with our previous knowledge (that Irena was behind her), we expect the threat to come from behind, even though we can't see it. In this way our attentions have been **Misdirected** so that when the bus enters from the front, we are completely unsuspecting of it.

Cat People sets up a situation in which we have an expectation of the outcome (violence, physical or verbal) that is predicated on dramatic irony, we then have our seat of informed knowledge challenged (our privileged position of knowing disappears with Irena), and finally our attention is misdirected from the "threat." Our expectation primes our tension; because we have an expectation for the scene, we experience it through the emotion of our expectations. We are unnerved when we realise that we are thrust into the same unknowing as Alice; we had thought ourselves privileged and so our emotions were for a fear of Alice but have now grown to include a fear of what the film will do to us.

Our misdirected attention combines with our emotions, we are looking for danger in the street behind Alice—and looking for small changes that signal danger are what our brains were programmed to do—so we are unprepared entirely when that "danger" comes from the direction we've neglected. In *Cat People* that danger was in fact safety, thankfully for Alice, and it further demonstrates a play against our expectations—we expected violence, not safety. This play against expectations may be read as an endorsement of the fake-out scare but the fake-out scare has been done often enough as to be part of the expectations the crowd brings into a horror film these days—it's not 1942, anymore.

Some jump scares work entirely by building off the element of surprise, such as Bob's death in *Halloween*. However, let's take a brief look at two of the most famous jump scare endings of horror history: *Friday the 13th* and *Carrie*. In *Friday the 13th*, a madwoman goes on a killing spree to avenge the drowning death of her son which she blames on the negligence of the camp counselors that were supposed to be watching him. She manages to kill all of the counselors except for Alice, who is able to behead the crazed Pamela Voorhees and rows out to the middle of the lake to wait until morning in a canoe.

The morning light illuminates the film, indeed it wasn't even this bright the day before when everything was still fun and games. The police arrive as hopeful music lilts across the soundtrack. She's save, she survived the night, and as she reflects on what this means and allows herself to feel safe for the first time, a hand falling to caress the surface of the water—A DEFORMED AND MUCK COVERED CHILD LEAPS OUT OF THE LAKE AND PULLS HER IN!

In *Carrie*, a bullied girl with psychic powers lashed out in a moment of anger, confusion, and pain, causing the deaths of everyone at the school prom and ending in the murder-suicide of her mother (which also causes the crumbling of her house). We then turn to Sue's mother who leaves her daughter's side to answer a phone call. Sue was a survivor of the night, she had tried to treat Carrie well and it was Sue that got Carrie to attend the prom in the first place. Sue's mother, thankful that the caller is a family friend and not a reporter, says that Sue is sleeping too much but that is to be expected. We then fade into Sue's dream: Sue carries a bouquet of flowers, herself dressed in a white dress that flows in the wind. She walks along a white picket fence and turns in at the gate, entering onto the property where the White house had once stood.

The debris has been cleared away and a wooden burial cross rests in the ground; only, we see when Sue gets closer, this isn't a burial cross but a "For Sale" sign shaped like a cross and with "Carrie White burns in hell!" written over it. The S of burns trails off into an arrow that points towards the base of the cross. Sue takes her time approaching, calm music playing on the soundtrack, we get the feeling that this is Sue's way of letting go (a reading we're primed for by her mother's mention that she wouldn't let her attend the funerals). Sue gently lays the flowers down, only the moment before they touch the earth—A BLOODY HAND BURSTS FORTH AND GRABS SUES WRIST; THE MUSIC BLARES; AND SUE WAKES UP SCREAMING IN HER MOTHER'S ARMS.

Friday the 13th and *Carrie* are both examples of a punch to the gut ending, a hook to catch the audience before they leave the theatre. I use them both as examples because Sean S. Cunningham has spoken about the end of *Friday the 13th* and how it was inspired by the ending of *Carrie*. They both use misdirection in order to trick the audience—this isn't a misdirection of look one way, BOO from the other, though. Here we are misdirected into thinking that the situation is over, the horror is now in the past. We have been misdirected on a story level, rather than on the level of an individual scene—but the core idea of misdirection is the same: figure out the audience expectation, misdirect them to further their expectations, then shock them when their guard is down.

Jump scares such as these can be handled in the writing phase: **identify what is expected and follow it by the unexpected**. There are some jump scares which gain their power in the edit, of course. A good example of this is in *The Exorcist III: Legion*. There is a quiet moment late at night in the hospital that the film is primarily set in. A young nurse is doing her rounds. We hold on a long shot of the hallway, capturing the nurse's desk at the far end. This shot is interrupted only sparingly, one or two cutaways to a point of view shot and one brief fake-out scare in one of the patients' rooms. But we keep cutting back to that same long shot. We watch the nurse go into one room, hold on the shot of the hall, see her come out, close the door, turn and walk away when—SHE IS SUDDENLY FOLLOWED BY FIGURE DRAPED IN WHITE CARRYING GARDENING SHEARS, READY TO DECAPITATE HER!

Here we see a moment that requires the editing, the holding of that shot for unnervingly long, in order to have the power that it does. But the editing can be suggested in the script stage, too. Going against traditional screenwriting advice, screenwriter William Peter Blatty uses a shocking fifteen lines in a single action paragraph in which he describes in painfully boring detail how the nurse goes about her rounds. When we are Scream Writing, we know that a paragraph of action represents a single shot.

A good Scream Writer uses this knowledge to play with the pacing and editing of their scene and that's what

Blatty did here in *The Exorcist III*. As dull as it is to read, we see it as a single shot, a single setup, and as we read it we grow bored and anxious and want something—anything!—to break up the monotony. It does in five quick lines that show us the door flying open, lets us hear "SHRIEK OF SCORE," leaves us with "a figure with a bed sheet draped over him and the decapitating shears thrust forward at neck level." Then we cut before the shears tear flesh. In his writing Blatty controls what he expects out of the cinematography and the pacing of the scene, and this vision was carried from the writing through to the edit.

Again, we see our expectations bite us in the ass: the nurse closes the door of the room she just exited, so she must not have seen anything in the room because her manner remains calm. The room is safe—indeed, the hallway must be safe, too; what kind of killer would strike in a hallway that sees a lot of foot traffic as opposed to a dark room with the door closed? But the figure does come from the room, the killer does strike in the hallway, all that we expect was wrong—we are shown how our expectations led us astray in a shocking moment that is this writer's all time favorite jump scare.

Decoy Protagonists and Hero Reversals

Now let's talk about the real shockers. These aren't just sudden moments and loud noises. We're getting into the shocks that really challenge you, the shocks that completely change the way you look at a movie or at the world.

When *Psycho* was released in 1960, it was truly a shock when the lead character was killed off around the 50 minute mark. This was a shocking scene at the time in the first place—it did depict the horrible death by stabbing of a naked woman in the shower—but the real power came from challenging the expectations of cinema goers. Marion Crane was the leading lady! Sure, she had some problems. She did steal money from her boss, after all. But she had a change of heart and was going to do the right thing! You don't just kill off your lead character, I mean … you can't … can you? Alfred Hitchcock knew that audiences would *never* expect it. They had been trained on what to expect from a Hollywood movie and this just … well … this just wasn't what happens, damnit!

Again, we see shock predicated on expectation. But this isn't about getting us to look right and hitting us from the left. This came from understanding what the audience expects from the cinema as a whole. It was used again in 1996 by Kevin Williamson in *Scream*. But because *Psycho* already existed, *Scream* had to work even harder to pull it off. The promo material heavily featured Drew Barrymore, who was then starting to make waves in a series of films and throughout entertainment media for her appearance in *Playboy* and for flashing David Letterman live on *The Late Show*. Drew Barrymore was starting to be a big name and she was plastered all over the promo material ... people were shocked to see her dead by the end of the first scene—it was *Psycho* all over again.

Unfortunately, pulling another *Psycho* shocker is going to be a helluva hard feat to pull off. Horror movie audiences have strong memories and there has been a string of movies that have handled it with less success. The **Decoy Protagonist** also shares similar DNA with the **Hero Reversal**, except that with the Hero Reversal we are first led to believe in the capability of the character who takes the role of hero. *The Stepfather* (1987) introduces Jim Ogilvie, brother out for vengeance against the man that murdered his sister—only to be killed off before he can even whip out his pistol. *Friday the 13th: The Final Chapter* (1984) has rugged badass Rob Dier, who dies screaming "He's killing me!" over and over again as he is hacked to death with a garden claw. *Freddy's Dead: The Final Nightmare* (1991) leads the audience (and the characters) to believe that John Doe is Freddy's son; turns out he actually had a daughter. The Hero Reversal has more power than the Decoy Protagonist does due to its (usually) late introduction into the film—it's easier to trick the audience when they've had more time to invest themselves into the character.

However, handled poorly and it is just that: a trick, not a shock. So handle your Decoy Protagonists and your Hero Reversals with care—if you understand how you have been leading the audience, which misdirections they will expect and which they won't, you will have a better chance at shocking them.

Endings, Expectations, and Emotions

Our studies on shock have shown us how important audience expectations are to achieving an effect, an emotional response. This section will finish our discussion on shock by focusing on shocking endings. I hadn't set out to focus on endings themselves but when I made my list I realized that each of the examples that I wanted to use leave their biggest shocks for last. Why is this?

For one, a shocking ending allows the audience to spend the absolute most time possible growing attached to the story and the characters and, as we've seen with fear, it is our attachment to characters that allows us to fully engage with a film on an emotional level. Part of this comes from the **Mirroring Effect** we see in psychology—human beings mirror each other's behaviour; so much so that tests have been performed in which scientists studied which parts of the brain lit up when a human being watched another human perform a task and compared them to when they watched a robot. Watching the robot did not provoke the mirroring behaviour but watching another human being did. From this we can see that one way to connect to an audience is by having a character experience the same emotions that we want the audience to experience. You'll notice that most of the examples of shocking endings covered here include characters able to react to the shock.

Another reason that these turned out to be endings is what is called the **Serial-Position Effect**. Coined in 1885 by the German psychologist Hermann Ebbinghaus, what the Serial-Position Effect says (in layman's terms) is that people remember best the first and last items in a list. We're Scream Writers, so we're not asking audiences to remember complicated lists but we are presenting them a story that flows in chronological order (in the audience's viewing of the film if not necessary the plot of the film itself). This tells us that the two most important points of our screenplays are the opening and the closing—an old piece of screenwriting advice reiterates this: the opening is the most important part for getting passed studio readers; the ending is the most important part for getting audiences to recommend it to friends. Because our opening introduces us to the world, we are not able to seed a powerful shock there—we might depict something shocking like a bombing or a sudden murder, but this event sets up the rules of our story world and a true shock requires those rules (and our characters) to be in place. If the opening is out, that means the ending is in.

The ending is the single most powerful moment that a film can have a shock—and one that truly sticks with the audience, one that challenges them on a fundamental level.

When *The Exorcist* was released in 1973, Roger Ebert referred to it as a "raw and painful experience" and questioned why people would go see it (as "enjoyment" and "delicious chills" were lacking). The film was shocking for many reasons. The special effects were gruesome and believable, for one. But even more than special effects was the corruption of a little girl … and not just in the movie: the horrible things they made that actress say! (Note, the swearing was done by voice actress Mercedes McCambridge and inclusion of her credit required an arbitration through the Screen Actors Guild). But most shocking of all was the down beat ending that left many viewers believing that evil had won.

The battle for the soul of a young girl is fought between the demon possessing her and the two Jesuit priests that attempt the titular exorcism. The older, more experienced priest dies during the exorcism and it's up to the younger Father Karras to see the battle against evil through to the end. And what an end it was! Karras challenges the demon to take him instead of the girl and then flings himself out of a window to tumble to his death down the flight of stairs next to the house. The shocking power of this ending comes from the original theatrical ending and its ambiguity.

While the 2000 "Version You've Never Seen" has a more upbeat ending. The atheist police detective forges a relationship with Father Dyer (a friend of Karras who was able to administer his last rites) and this implies the detective's soon-to-be conversion to Christianity. But in the original ending, there is none of the hopefulness that author William Peter Blatty intended the film to have and years later he would tell a story about how disappointed he was in the ending and the fact that people didn't realize it was supposed to end on a positive note—he described venting this frustration to a friend that then confessed he hadn't realized it was a happy ending either.

The shock of this ending isn't in the death of Father Karras itself but in the ambiguity. *The Exorcist* is a religious film, through and through. It charts the battle of good against evil, of capital g God against capital d Devil. What's more is this battle is fought through the body of an innocent child—the Devil chooses a battlefield that suggests hopelessness and the barbarity of true evil. In the Christian mind, God must win—absolutely and thoroughly, no shadow of a doubt. The fact that the film left the victor undecided was truly troubling and shocking to the core, a challenge to the fundamental beliefs of Christian viewers (not to be mistaken as "a challenge to fundamental Christians"). The shock arises out of religious expectation—that God will win—and it leaves the audience with a lasting emotional experience that requires them to question what they've witnessed and find their own answers.

The Exorcist shocked religious sensibilities but it's true that for non-religious people this shock was not nearly so profound. In our remaining examples of fundamental shock, we will explore how *The Mist* (2007) shocks the logical, how *Pitstop* (1969) shocks us through character identification (a tactic used expertly in *Henry: Portrait of a Serial Killer*), and how *It Comes at Night* (2017) shocks us through human nature and the existential meaningless of violence.

The Mist is the story of a small town that is suddenly cloaked in a thick cloud of mist. David Drayton happens to be shopping with his son, Billy, and, along with a couple dozen other people, is trapped in the supermarket when the mist overtakes the town. An injured man rushes out of the mist, yelling and screaming that there are creatures in the mist that took his friend. Finding out first hand that there are indeed monsters in the mist, and that they are trapped, the group slowly begins to break into two: on one side is the religious Mrs. Carmody, a deeply pious woman that believes God is punishing them; on the other side is David, who believes deeply in thinking logically in order to survive the situation. As tensions rise, more people begin to follow Mrs. Carmody as her predictions and proclamations start happening for real—this leads to human sacrifice and forces David's group to take drastic action: they shoot Mrs. Carmody (in order to prevent the sacrifice of two of their group, including the young Billy) and dash through the parking lot where five of them are able to escape in a car.

The group drives until they run out of gas, never able to escape from the mist. Stuck, the group agrees to suicide—except for the young Billy, his father deciding for him. With only four bullets and five people, David agrees to shoot the others and let himself be taken by the monsters. He exits the car and screams to be taken, a deep rumbling letting him and the audience know that they are close. Flame cuts through the mist, military vehicles and soldiers pour forth, fighting a winning battle against the monsters and clearing away the mist—in the back of a military transport truck are the survivors from the supermarket, safe from harm. David collapses to the ground, only capable of screaming in grief, the suicide of his friends and the murder of his son all for nothing.

The Mist offers a disturbing and shocking ending. First, the realization that the group and his son were killed when they were moments away from safety is a helluva gut punch. The realization of the pointlessness of the deaths is shocking but even more shocking is the lingering image of this realization setting in for David. David's realization serves to offer audiences a character through which to experience the psychological effects of mirroring. If all the power that *The Mist* holds was confined to this one scene, it would still go down as one of the most shocking endings in film history, but this ending is built off the events of the previous two hours in such a devious way—it manages to confront the audience with the fallibility of logic.

Throughout the film, the character of David grows into a leadership position among his small handful of followers because of his logical approach to the situation. David is not one to give into the emotional responses of those around him, nor does he ever take the threat lightly or allow himself to drop his guard. At all times, David makes his choices through a logical process that endears him to the audience.

As viewers, we don't want to be asked to identify with a moron—we make fun of the character in a slasher movie that goes into the dark room or, as *Scream* mentioned, runs up the stairs when they should be going out the front door. As audiences, we want characters whose choices are similar to or reflect our own—or, rather, reflect how we would like to imagine our own. Through his logical approach, David stands in for the audience as a projection of ourselves—and that's what makes the ending so damn powerful and shocking.

David's logic … our logic … failed. We thought that we were making the right choices, we thought that the world adhered to logic and that we could think our way through it. Yes, not every choice was perfect—I mean, Ollie did die in the parking lot while trying to escape—but damnit, logic dictates that there will be some loss of life and the risk was weighed against the reward. But in the end … logic wasn't enough. *The Mist* carries such a shock not just because of the nature of the events that make up the ending but because the ending is a cruel reminder that the world is chaotic and any attempt to apply logic and order to it is a temporary bastion of the mind against this knowledge.

Pitstop is not itself a horror movie but its ending is so shocking that I couldn't help but include it (with the hopes that more people will watch it). The movie centers on Rick Bowman, a young hotshot driver that gets involved in figure-eight stock car racing. Throughout the film we grow attached to Rick, his mistakes become understandable—a little frustrating, sure (we do want to see him grow and learn of course), but understandable. That is, until the final minutes of the film. Rick's responsible for the crash of a teammate. He goes to see him at the hospital but the man's already dead from a broken neck. All of Rick's friends are in tears and angry, but Rick doesn't show any emotion. Rick's told he has to get going, career duties call, and he leaves without saying a word— the pain and misery of his 'friends' having no meaning to him.

Pitstop works to create the same kind of shock that *Henry: Portrait of a Serial Killer* generates. Both of these films introduce us to characters that we see acting horribly, yet we find ourselves drawn to them and investing in the idea that they will grow. *Henry* does this by contrasting the main character with the disgusting Otto—*Pitstop* contrasts Rick with the loose cannon, aggressive Hawk Sidney; except Hawk grows to be more likable throughout the movie—we realize that behind his bluster and posturing is a deeply emotional human being; Otto was always an asshole.

The early contrast in *Pitstop* is enough to carry the audience's investment through the 'mistakes' that Rick makes in the second half: he cheats on his girl and he sets up his partner. He is so full of himself and we keep waiting for the moment where he realizes the error of his ways; hell, we saw Hawk change so why can't Rick? We have every expectation that Rick is about to learn a lesson the hard way when he walks into the emergency room and the trap door is dropped out from under us so quickly that we barely have time to understand what's just happened before the movie's done. *Pitstop* shocks us by leading those expectations and then confronting us with the fact that Rick has changed. He's changed for the worse because winning means more to some people than basic human decency

Finally, let's talk about *It Comes at Night*. I wrote about how the film sets up a perfect opening scene for the Scream Writing column on Scriptophobic.ca and highly recommend reading the screenplay. However, the screenplay has a much different (and longer) ending than the movie. The movie was able to cut thirty minutes from the projected running time and, in doing so, it found the much more shocking ending. *It Comes at Night* manages to shock because of the level of violence, the uselessness of it, and it manages to wrap these shocks within a blanket of mood: depression, sorrow, and futility. Because *It Comes at Night* is so effective, I have to recommend watching the film before reading this section—it's a downer but a damned powerful one.

The film centers on Paul, Sarah, and Travis—husband, wife, and son. The family lives in a boarded up house with no running electricity, secluded in the middle of the woods. We come to understand that there is some kind of illness that has affected the world, and Paul looks after his family with a stomach made of iron. Paranoia runs strong and when a man tries to break into the home, they take him hostage until they can see he isn't carrying the illness. He proves to be healthy, a family man just trying to find some water to look after his own. Paul and Sarah agree to bring his family to stay with them, the more hands the easier to defend (plus he said they have plenty of food), and so Will, Kim, and young Andrew, come to stay with them.

Fresh faces around the house bring a resurgence of life to the downtrodden monotony and for a time everything is good. When the family dog escapes into the woods, Travis chases after but is unable to catch him. That night, Travis can't sleep and goes for a late night walk around the house. He finds Andrew asleep on the floor of Grandpa's room and takes him back to his parents' room. Travis hears an odd noise that catches his attention and follows it to the one door that leads to the outside. Normally locked at all times, the door is slightly open and, when something bangs against the other side, Travis wakes his parents to investigate. The dog is back but he's sick and dying and this raises the question: who opened the door?

A tense dinner table meeting reveals that Andrew was awake and might have opened it but the kid can't remember. No one is sure what happened and everyone agrees when Paul suggests that each family take enough supplies for a couple days and quarantine themselves in their respective rooms. Awoken by nightmares again, Travis takes a visit to the attic cubby hole that he used to listen into his parents' and Will's room. Travis hears Andrew coughing, sounding very sick. He wakes his parents and tells them what he heard, that Andrew sounds sick and he thinks they are preparing to leave.

Paul and Sarah know this isn't an option, if they grow desperate then they may come back and attack them for their supplies. Paul tries to confront Will but gets taken hostage at gunpoint. Sarah frees Paul, who struggles with

Will, and chases after Kim and Andrew, catching up to them before they can get out of the house. Paul and Sarah take the hostages out into the woods, Sarah growing more unsure about their actions with every step, Kim growing more scared. Will manages to get the drop on Paul and as he's brutally beating him, Sarah shoots him. Kim runs with Andrew in her arms. Paul fires a shot at her but hits Andrew instead, killing him. Kim's cries of anguish turn into demands to be killed. Paul shoots her, then realizes that Will is still alive and shoots him dead too.

This shocking level of violence builds off the tension of the preceding scenes and manages to be shocking in its intensity as Will beats Paul's face to a bloody pulp. The death of young Andrew carries the weight that the death of any child does—innocence being brutally murdered stands against our cultural values—but the fact that, like *The Mist*, the film lingers on the anguish of the parent gives the scene its true shocking power. Because horror films so often ignore the emotional aspect of death—how rare it is to see funerals and grieving—seeing grief on screen plays against audience expectations.

But *It Comes at Night* isn't done there.

Will's family is dead but Travis is sick. He comes in and out of consciousness to see his mother comforting him—without her gloves and mask. She promises that everything will be okay. But the last shot returns us to the dining room table, the spot where Travis once sat is now empty and Paul and Sarah can only sit in silence across from each other. The film cuts to black and we realize that they, too, must be infected and the image we've just seen is two people waiting for death. The film doesn't just give us shocking, disturbing violence.

The film gives us shocking, disturbing, and ultimately pointless violence. And it makes us feel sick—throughout the film Paul has been rational and, though he has a hard edge to him, it's hard not to find yourself agreeing with him more often than not. That the agreement led to disgusting, disturbing violence and that that violence was absolutely meaningless in the end? There's a sense of mistrust instilled in us, in our own thoughts and logic, but there's also the blunt acknowledgement that violence doesn't have a purpose—violence isn't reasonable, violence can explode out of nowhere, without a purpose, without a point, without anything. *It Comes at Night* confronts us with the shocking truth that violence is just violence and violence is always shocking.

With jump scares, we saw how expectation and misdirection are key to shocking the audience out of their seats in a manner that relieves emotional tension. By understanding both the audience's cultural expectations and those you build as Scream Writers, as well as understanding how to direct their attention and how to misguide it, we can craft wonderful jumpscares that feel earned in an honest manner rather than leave the audience feeling cheated.

We discussed how these tools can be used to craft Decoy Protagonists and Hero Reversals. Finally, we've seen how a film can gain power by using its ending to shock and how these shocks play on more than just the events (a priest dying, a needless suicide, pointless violence, etc.) but generate shocks that challenge the audience on a fundamental level by building off theme and plot. We now know that shocks work on several levels, so we can now choose which shocks best help generate the cognitive effect we want from the audience.

Disgust

Disgust closes out our discussion of the primary tools that define horror. Unlike shock and fear, disgust is easier to understand and has less bells and whistles. Disgust is a profound disapproval or revulsion. Our natural action when faced with something disgusting is to distance ourselves from the object or to close our eyes in an attempt to cut it off at the cognitive source, our senses. In our lives we have to deal with the experience of disgust assaulting all five of our senses, whereas, on film, disgust is primarily a function of vision and thought, sometimes extending through hearing. In order to understand how we can make use of disgust, let us first explore the visual and audio element of disgust.

If you were to think of something that disgusts you, it is likely you will turn first to an object like rotting food, fecal matter, vomit, and the like. After the most prevalent examples of visual stimuli, you might expand on these to include smells, such as the smell of shit or rot, or sounds, such as those of vomiting. Our senses are intricately linked to each other, so much so that oftentimes a disgusting location in film, when described by an audience member or critic, will make reference to the perceived smell of the location.

This linkage between our senses allows us as Scream Writers to focus on the visual stimuli, secure in the knowledge that it will overcome the limitations of two-dimension screen space and assault the viewer on a multi-sensual level. This means that the visual—and to a lesser degree, the audio—level carries the weight of not only what is shown but the memories the image provokes. Sound, such as a person that is vomiting off screen, will provoke the image of the action (and the smell) in the same way that depicting the event will—however, our strongest sense tends to be our visual, so showing leads to a more assaultive experience.

We are disgusted by objects because of the feelings of abjection they provoke. As discussed in the previous chapter, abjection represents a threatened breakdown between the self and the other. Let us think of this self not as our physical bodies (though that is most certainly a part of it) but as our mental representations of the world, as well. Rotten fruit and meat serves to remind the viewer of the realities of having a body—that is, we think of ourselves as beings and not as sacks of meat that will one day rot. Rotten food provokes similar feelings to the disgust and abjection that is felt when we watch a movie about cannibals—we are not food, we are people, but to them we are just meat and this threatens a breakdown in how we view ourselves.

Of course, the most common way to provoke disgust and objection within the horror film is through the mutilation of the human body. It isn't just body horror that focuses on our complicated (and often delusional) relationship with our bodies. The slasher film, the serial killer film, the cannibal film, the monster movie, just about (but not quite) every form of the horror film confronts the audience with images of the destruction of the human form. Even *Freaks* (1932) focused on provoking abjection in the viewer by confronting the audience with real life human oddities (thankfully, however, director Tod Browning pulled from his own experiences working in the circus to bring a depth of compassion and love to his characters).

We can also see abjection at play when it comes to disgust in the form of ideas. This form of disgust might be achieved by confronting the audience with ideas that run counter to their world view (such as the idea that torture is acceptable, or that pleasure can be found within human misery). Unlike the visual form of disgust, **Intellectual Disgust** can be achieved merely through dialogue, a character exploring ideas that are revolting to the audience for example. Of course, plot events and outcomes, images, sounds, all of these are tools that can help to strengthen this form of disgust as well. However, this is a form of disgust that requires ideas and not just the visual image or the sound of someone vomiting because this form of disgust happens not within the senses but within the mind itself and can actually be strengthened on reflection.

One example comes in the form of young Linda Blair in *The Exorcist*. It was thought to be absolutely disgusting, the things they made that little girl do (masturbate with a crucifix and use such awful, horrendous language). Of course, we know now that Linda Blair did not do or say those things, they were created through movie magic. But the fact that little girls don't behave that way (or, rather, aren't supposed to behave that way according to the moral majority) disgusted the audiences because of the threatened breakdown in their worldview and the abjection this breakdown caused. When watching the film there is a level of disgust at what was being seen and heard that was then later deepened on reflection when the audience realized that they weren't just seeing a fictional little girl but an actress doing those things (thus furthering their abjection because the, perceived, reality also threatened this breakdown).

Visual disgust is often thought of as being a cheap way of provoking an emotional response in the audience. But if you understand what you are doing with it, it can be a powerful tool. Do you think Sloth or Gluttony would have been nearly as powerful in the film *Se7en* (1995) if it wasn't for the visual disgust they provoked? Would the dinner scene in *The Texas Chainsaw Massacre* be nearly as claustrophobic and harrowing if it wasn't for how disgusting that dining room looked? It wasn't just being trapped with this insane family, it was also where we were trapped and how that space made us feel.

Imagine if that scene was set in a school cafeteria, a nice upper-class home, or just about anywhere else except there. We would still be concerned about Sally's safety but we wouldn't feel as off center as we did if we were stuck somewhere nicer; that feeling of being surrounded by the disgusting and unable to escape just wouldn't be present and a level of power would be missing from our viewing experience. Likewise, think about the moment in *Green Room* (2015) when Pat pulls his mutilated arm back into the room. It was shocking, for sure, but it was also one of the most disgusting special effects in horror history and it was this feeling of disgust (combined, at the same time, with shock) that let us know we weren't safe in Jeremy Saulnier's film—we were in for a roller coaster ride and there was no telling where it was going to go next.

As much as visual disgust is thought of as being cheap, intellectual disgust is often ignored entirely. Because intellectual disgust lacks the primacy of shock, fear, and visual disgust, it often goes unnoticed in a direct fashion. However, even if the conscious brain does not realize that it is experiencing disgust, the subconscious brain absolutely does and this emotional effect will often be mixed into the more immediate feelings (in the language of the viewer). It's important to understand that even if it isn't vocalized, intellectual disgust is playing a strong part in the experience of the viewer, so we should never take it for granted. It is of the utmost importance that Scream Writers strive to understand the levels of intellectual disgust they are pushing their audience through; it is possible to carelessly provoke intellectual disgust and to do it for unintended and unbeneficial reasons.

Not a horror movie but the example that comes most immediately to mind is *The Searchers* (1956), a John Wayne western about tracking the Native Americans that kidnapped his niece. Racism is a strong component of the film, purposefully so, and it manages intellectual disgust on this level. There is a scene, however, in which a Native American woman is abused, which causes John Wayne to laugh—the character he is playing would laugh and that registers as disgusting (purposefully so) but the filmmakers show their lack of concern about the woman when they don't even deem her worthy of having a reaction to the situation. She is treated as a non-entity and this provokes unintended intellectual disgust directed not within the movie itself but at the filmmakers.

Disgust is a tool that can be easily used and abused. If a film sets out to provoke disgust as its primary cognitive effect, it will often fail to have a lasting impact. However, when disgust is combined with the other tools of the Scream Writer, it can serve to enhance the range of emotions generated in the audience in powerful ways. Understanding what is disgusting in our screenplays and why it is disgusting is of such paramount importance—if we don't understand the cognitive and emotional effects that we are provoking, we don't understand how we are leading the audience and we fail to achieve our desired effect; if we don't understand, we are not in control and Scream Writing is all about control.

Anxiety: Horror's Bread and Butter

As we discovered during our semantic exploration, one of the primary aspects of the Scream Writer's toolbox is the selection of tools designed to generate anxiety. Suspense, tension, dread, and unease are all anxiety provoking tools that work in conjunction with fear, shock, and disgust. The horror film is at its most powerful when it is combining tools together for cognitive effect rather than relying on any one tool on its lonesome. In this section we will explore these anxiety focused tools before we turn to atmosphere to close out the chapter.

Suspense and Tension

These two terms are often used interchangeably but there are important differences. Suspense is, according to the *Oxford Dictionary*, "a state or feeling of excited or anxious uncertainty about what may happen." The key piece of the puzzle is found in the "about what may happen" bit at the end. Suspense requires the audience to feel about what may happen, rather than what has or is happening. Tension, on the other hand, is "mental or emotional strain; intense suppressed suspense, anxiety, or excitement."

From the sounds of it, tension is generated through suspense—except notice that it isn't just suspense, it is suppressed suspense. Further, tension doesn't require something to happen, tension can just be. For example, think of the tension that would be nearly palpable at the breakfast table the morning after a conservative father caught his son red-handed smoking drugs—there is no suspense, the "will he, won't he" of getting caught has already happened, but there is now tension, there is emotional strain affecting the family's conversation, body language, and the general mood.

In the book *Hitchcock: A Definitive Study of Alfred Hitchcock* by François Truffaut, director Alfred Hitchcock delivered a famous example of how suspense differs from surprise. Let us look at it now to see a perfect example of suspense:

> We are now having a very innocent little chat. Let's suppose that there is a bomb underneath this table between us. Nothing happens, and then all of a sudden, "Boom!" There is an explosion. The public is surprised, but prior to this surprise, it has seen an absolutely ordinary scene, of no special consequence. Now, let us take a suspense situation. The bomb is underneath the table and the public knows it, probably because they have seen the anarchist place it there. The public is aware the bomb is going to explode at one o'clock and there is a clock in the decor. The public can see that it is a quarter to one. In these conditions, the same innocuous conversation becomes fascinating because the public is participating in the scene.

The audience is longing to warn the characters on the screen: "You shouldn't be talking about such trivial matters. There is a bomb beneath you and it is about to explode!" In the first case we have given the public fifteen seconds of surprise at the moment of the explosion. In the second we have provided them with fifteen minutes of suspense.

This is a great example of making the audience feel suspense but Hitchcock failed to elaborate on how this also generates tension. The audience is in suspense because they know what will happen, they have an event they are concerned about. The definition of suspense refers to an "uncertainty about what may happen," so it may seem that Hitchcock's example of suspense actually precludes the possibility of suspense—after all, the audience knows the bomb will go off at one. It is absolutely a description of dramatic irony but is it suspense?

Yes, absolutely.

Even though the audience knows the bomb will go off at one, they don't know if the characters will still be seated at the table, they will be hanging on, hoping that they leave (if they like the characters). They will be in a state of suspense not of the event itself (the bomb going off) but of the outcome of the event (our heroes living or dying). So Hitchcock is absolutely right, this is a way to generate suspense. But what about the tension he overlooked?

Tension is a state of mental or emotional strain, yes, but it is also a state of suppressed suspense. Interestingly, Hitchcock's example generates its tension through its suspense. The characters are having a conversation, we are in a state of suspense about the bomb going off; however, the film suppresses this suspense by focusing on the innocuous conversation. Where a film like *The Man Who Knew Too Much* (1956) builds suspense around a question of "will he, won't he" regarding an assassination plot, the characters are aware of it and so the film focuses on suspense but without tension; meanwhile, a look at any of the *Friday the 13th* films demonstrates tension through dramatic irony—we know a killer is on the loose, we are in on the dramatic irony, but we are also in a state of suspense because of this dramatic irony; but we're also experiencing a level of tension because our identification characters are either oblivious to the situation or are forced to suppress their anxieties, their gut feelings that something isn't right, and this (with the filmmaking) suppresses the suspense into tension.

Suspense is the easier of the two cognitive effects to generate; dramatic irony is almost always a form of generating suspense (though it can be used for comedy and tragedy as well). Because suspense is linked to an event happening, one way to generate suspense is through clever foreshadowing. If we are given hints towards what may happen, that the event will be bad, we will begin to experience a feeling of suspense. In this way foreshadowing points towards an unknown outcome (unless it telegraphs itself far too plainly), while dramatic irony points towards a suspected outcome.

Despite both being suspense, these two forms of generation give rise to different feelings—dramatic irony lets us know the event we're feeling suspense for, it's a clearer and altogether less unpleasant feeling of suspense. But foreshadowing, if it's able to keep you in the dark, leaves its event as an unknown—if it's unknown to us, we attempt to tell ourselves that we know what will happen, we've been here before as horror movie viewers, it's silly to feel this suspense … we try to suppress it and in doing so give rise to a feeling of tension, a deeper suspense. Suppression of suspense weighs heavily on our emotional and mental processes—something that tension makes good use of.

Tension also has the dual meaning of "mental or emotional strain." How can we use this? Our example of the strain around the conservative breakfast table works for identifying what we mean but as horrible as living through it is, it isn't really horror movie fodder. But what about the movie *Green Room*? Tons of suspense, you know that the band has to get out and the Nazis want to get in and kill them. It's very clear the root of the suspense, it's not even close to suppressed, so where's the tension?

Anyone that's seen the film knows it is a tense, tense, tense ride that leaves your stomach in knots. This comes from that mental or emotional strain. The film never lets up, the situation doesn't relax, the audience never gets a chance to feel safe, nor do the characters. They are trapped in a situation that is absolutely filled with mental and emotional strain—they are under attack, they are stuck, they have no hope, they are outnumbered … all of these weigh heavy on the emotions (fear, anger, sadness, hopelessness, anxiety, etc.) and the mind (the thought of what will happen, having to try to think of a way out, having to try to think of a way to escape while fighting against these emotions).

Where suspense is an anticipation, tension is an assault.

Atmosphere

We saw that when we explore what we mean by atmosphere of a piece, what we are actually talking about is a combination of tone and mood. We broke this down even further to see that this means atmosphere is made up of a combination of "the general character or attitude" (or, tone) and the "particular feeling or state of mind" (or mood) that exists throughout our screenplays and is elaborated on and expanded through cinematography, mise-en-scene, acting, lighting, editing, the whole package of production. Because so many parts come together to turn a screenplay into a feature film, you might think that, as a Scream Writer, atmosphere isn't a major concern of yours.

But like we saw Bill Lancaster do with the lighting in the screenplay for *The Thing*, we actually have more control as Scream Writers than it might at first appear. Mel Brooks once said "everything starts with writing," and he wasn't alone in identifying the power of the page; Akira Kurosawa said "With a good script, a good director can produce a masterpiece. With the same script, a mediocre director can produce a passable film. But with a bad script even a good director can't possibly make a good film."

Mind you, both Kurosawa and Brooks are writers so you might think them biased. But actors and directors have both reiterated the same point; actress Jessica Raine has said that "For any role, I pretty much always go to the script, first and foremost," and Ewan McGregor has said that "The script, I always believe, is the foundation for everything." In the words of Alex Garland, "Don't disregard the script … film sometimes neglects that and it does it to its detriment."

The power of the script is undeniable.

So you might think that atmosphere isn't your concern but you'd be doing a horrible disservice to your screenplay if you choose to disregard such a tremendous aspect of the story—atmosphere isn't just something that happens when our characters are wandering into the dark cabin that hides the killer. Atmosphere pervades every moment of the story we are telling, from the first frame until the credits roll (and sometimes even throughout and after them).

The "particular feeling or state of mind" of mood and the "general character or attitude" of tone are very similar to each other, so let's explore what we mean by each. A good way of separating the two is to think of tone as how the Scream Writer (you) feels and to think of mood as how the audience feels. In this way, our tone feeds into the overall mood and together this creates atmosphere. Earlier, I used *The Searchers* as an example of a film that disgusted me on an unintended level; I could describe this feeling of disgust by saying that the tone of the filmmakers affected my mood as a viewer—their lack of concern for the racialized woman disgusted me and the mood I was meant to feel was not disgust because it was supposed to be a humorous moment.

In this way, tone is able to affect mood but mood rarely affects tone. Both tone and mood are created through our choice of language and our staging of the plot but while it is of utmost importance to do our best to control the mood throughout our scripts (as I keep saying, over and over again), we don't have as direct control of mood as we do tone because each audience member brings their own experiences and perspectives with them into every film that they watch.

We aim to control mood by understanding the cognitive effects that we are generating in the audience (fear, shock, disgust, anxiety, etc.) and we've already explored these tools, but what about tone? Tone is created by what we focus on—if a character has just had a heartbreak, do you focus on that or do you move on to the next scene and completely ignore it? Well, the answer depends on what we want. Do we want a sympathetic tone? A detached tone? Maybe we're going for a darkly comedic tone and the juxtaposition of the next scene is designed for laughs. But tone isn't just what we focus on, it's how we focus on it, too. Do we want to share in the characters emotions and experience this heartbreak? Maybe want to spring off of them, create a tone of unrelenting negativity like in Brian De Palma's *Dressed to Kill* (1980)?

Stuck in an unloving relationship, Kate Miller has an extramarital tryst with a stranger she meets in a museum. Feeling refreshed, full of life, young again, Kate looks for a pen to write him a note and discovers a letter from his doctor that he has a sexually transmitted disease. This shocking revelation absolutely tears down the happiness that she was feeling earlier, the film has a tone of spitefulness, of ironic cruelty, and this creates an emotional reaction in the viewer. We feel disgusted by the uncaring coward for not telling her beforehand, saddened by the crumbling of her happiness, disgusted and afraid by the thought of this happening to us, worried about how this will effect Kate's home life and her already rocky marriage.

When Kate goes to leave the apartment building and gets brutally murdered in the elevator, that ironic cruelty has turned into unrelenting cruelty, the tone is even darker—it wasn't enough for Kate to die, she had to die at her lowest moment. Our moods fluctuate, we're disgusted (some of us at the graphic violence, some at the fact a filmmaker and screenwriter were completely in control and chose to put Kate through this), our hearts go out to her and, having just experience such a profound moment of shock with her, we are filled with pity and anger and a sense of the chaotic, random, uncaring nature of the world. Our moods are influenced by both the event (her murder) itself and by the tone (cruelty, irony, spitefulness) that surrounds and composes the event.

Tone is captured on the page by every choice we make. What scene we put where, how that scene plays out, what we choose to focus on with our action paragraphs, what we choose not to focus on … Every choice we make as Scream Writers feeds into the tone of our stories and this includes our choice of words, too. We're able to inject a wider depth of feeling into our screenplays when we carefully choose the right word for the situation. But the very fact that we have decided on this word or that word contributes to our tone. The perfect word might not be the most concise but actually the one that conveys how you, the Scream Writer, feel and how you want others to feel.

Atmosphere is more than just tone and mood, through both of these are absolutely key. Atmosphere also arises out of the events (which themselves are governed by tone and mood) but also by the settings. Settings carry complicated and extensive emotional baggage with them that affects atmosphere—baggage that we should consider when writing out screenplays and so let us turn our attention to those next.

Exercises

1. List out the four or five moments you consider to be the scariest in all of horror. Take note of whether they use tension, disgust, fear, or shock. Examine how the filmmakers brought these elements into the scene to scare you.

2. Take a look at your most atmospheric sequences. What words are being used in these sections? Can they be strengthened by exploring connotation? Are they suggesting mood in and of themselves? In order to properly convey atmosphere, we need to have a solid grasp on the language of these sequences, using words that suggest hidden layers, the quality of the lighting and sound.

3. Have you built any jump scares into your Scream Play? Have you earned them? Does your language misdirect the viewers attention? Do they arise naturally from the situation or are they being forced through unconvincing circumstances?

4. The story has been building to the ending this whole time, have you considered not just what happens in the end but how you want the audience to feel? Is this where the action gets cranked up the 10 and the audience isn't given a chance to breathe? Is there a twist? If so, are we

supposed to be just surprised, shocked, confused, disappointed, terrified, saddened, or humored?

Chapter 4: Settings

What I see as the particularly exciting prospect for writing horror ... is setting stories in more internal landscapes than external ones, mapping out the mind as the home for scary things instead of the house at the end of the lane or lakeside campground or abandoned amusement park.

Andrew Pyper

The Legend of Hell House (1973), The Overlook Hotel from *The Shining, House on Haunted Hill* (1959, 1999), the *Event Horizon* (1997), the cave in *The Descent*, the Bates Motel, the base camp in *The Thing*, the catacombs of Paris in *As Above, So Below* (2014), *The Cabin in the Woods* (2012), the titular *Green Room*, the gothic castles of Hammer Film Productions, the lakeside getaway of *Funny Games,* the Nostromo in *Alien*, the beaches of Jean Rollin ... Horror is nothing if not well traveled and cosmopolitan.

Preparation for this chapter revealed how little has been written about settings in regards to both screenwriting in general and the horror screenplay specifically. The Script Lab's Eric Owusu writes that "writing a great setting simply means effectively conveying in your screenplay where your characters are, what period of time they exist in, or what universe they're in, without droning on and on about details that don't interestingly relate to your characters, their situations, or the advancement of the plot." While his point is focused on the need for brevity within our screenplays, it implies that setting is unimportant and only exists to surround the action of the story.

Setting, Owusu seems to be saying, is the milk in the bowl of cereal. It surrounds everything but should not be the focus. But what he is missing is the importance of the milk itself. That bowl of cereal wouldn't be worth a damn if the milk were spoiled or motor oil. Setting description may require brevity but the setting itself is as important, in Scream Writing, as our monsters and scares. The cognitive effects we generate are not done in a void—so let's not treat our settings as such.

Instead, let's work to understand how we can leverage our settings to help us affect our audiences, to bring them into the emotional crevices we seek to guide them. In order to do this we must understand audience expectations and explore what has been done "to death," and look at ways of breathing new life into those locations. Expectation is tied into the psychological baggage that festers inside locations and it plays a part in shaping our experience when it comes to places of disempowerment. We'll examine how some locations become characters in their own right and how a location can actually serve as a threat to propel conflict. Finally, we'll take a look at isolation and confinement to explore the cross sections between setting and plot.

Walking in Circles: The Overused Locations of Horror

The manor rests on the top of a steep incline, a driveway like a tentacle curling down to meet the rusted gate that separates the family's domain from the main road. A small village, the locals secretive and afraid, the final resting place for weary travelers to get a bite to eat before pushing on to the gloomy castle in the mountains, perpetually cast in the deepest of shadows. The hospital corridor that seems endless when the light of day fades. The summer camp that holds a deadly secret. So often we have seen the settings of horror be repeated in film after film, one might be inclined to agree with *Halloween: Resurrection* (2002)'s Rick Rosenthal when he said on the commentary track that "you have to have a spooky house."

We have seen our fair share of haunted houses, gothic castles, haunted hotels, creepy farm houses, stalked summer camps, dorms dripping blood, and just *so* many cabins in the woods.

Is it necessary for a horror film to follow in the footsteps of its predecessors?

Absolutely not and we'll touch on breathing new life in a moment. But it's important to look at why we see the same places used so often.

Partly, it is a case of copying what worked. *Friday the 13th* was a super successful film set at a summer camp, so *The Burning* (1981), *Madman* (1981), and *Sleepaway Camp* (1983) followed in its footsteps and copied its summer camp location. However, this is not just a case of monkey see, monkey do. There are also some clear advantages to the setting that lend themselves to crafting effective horror. We'll dig deeper into these later in the chapter but a quick look shows us that: these locations are cut off from the wider world, if help can get there at all (which it often can't due to stormy weather or phone lines being cut, etc.) it takes a fair chunk of time; not only is this an isolation from the wider world but there's an isolation between cabins and a level of confinement to the location due to the surrounding woods and the threat of getting lost within them; this isolation and confinement further feeds into a cognitive effect of disempowerment; and, finally, there is a level of social context placed on the counselors who represent the knowing adults, they are supposed to be in charge and responsible and there is a psychological tug-of-war within the characters between that responsible adult role and the role of the scared child.

Because these elements all serve to enhance the cognitive effect that we aim to produce in the audience, and these summer camps capture it so well, it's easy to see why the location has been used so often. A cabin in the woods is another great example, being even more cut off from the world—perhaps best reflected in *Evil Dead* with the destruction of the bridge; not only are the characters cut off from driving out but the woods themselves are evil and capable of killing.

These locations that have been used over and over again have been used for a reason. It's easier to see the benefits of using a location if that location has been explored in films of the past; standing on the shoulders of blood thirsty giants, as it were. But because they have been used so often, they have sunken into parody—there's no better example than *The Cabin in the Woods*, a film whose title parodies the well tread setting. But *The Cabin in the Woods* is also an inventive and clever horror-comedy fusion that breathes new life into the location.

When we discussed the Universal films of the 1930s, we saw how they represented the genre falling into parody and suffering a "crisis." But we also saw how short lived that crisis was before the genre found new life with the works of Val Lewton. I argue that settings face a similar pattern—we see a setting in a successful film be copied again and again until it loses its spark, only to be reclaimed by later filmmakers who challenge themselves to approach the location with creativity and innovation rather than simply tread the well worn path.

I refuse to give any advice that slots into a dichotomy of "do this, don't do this." Storytelling is too expansive, horror is too expansive, to have limitations placed on it. What I will say is to examine your settings. Think about what you've seen done with them before. Ask yourself what advantage the setting is giving you in generating that cognitive effect.

Ask yourself if there are other ways or other places that work better. Challenge yourself to think outside the box, to reinvent the summer camp, the hospital, or the cabin in the woods. Perhaps you'll see it's not the setting that's been done to death but the way it's been handled. Perhaps you'll be the one to breathe new life on the dying embers. Perhaps you'll be the one they copy next.

You Don't See There Everyday

Alien was an absolute masterpiece of terror. Partly, as we've seen, it was through the multilayered reveal of the evolving xenomorph. But let's not discredit the effect the setting had. Previously, science fiction and horror hadn't really been joined together. There were monsters from space like *The Blob* and *The Thing From Another World* (1951) but spacefaring science fiction had more in common with the adventure film than it did with horror. There were films with monsters on other planets, such as *The Angry Red Planet* (1960) and *Terrore nello Spazio* (*Planet of the Vampires*, 1965) but, again, these carried an almost Odyssey-like feeling—what sights the islands of mythology hold, transposed now against the ocean of space. *Alien* took the depths of space and drained away their glamour.

Borrowing from the style of Lovecraft, the alien planet that the crew visits has a depth of unanswered mystery to it—what exactly we are looking at is never fully understood. There's a gothic ambience that calls to mind the ruined castles of Hammer films. But the standout location is the spaceship Nostromo. Where previously the starships of science fiction were smooth chromatic vessels that spoke to the utopian advancements of science, the Nostromo is a brooding, claustrophobic maze of metallic pipes and yonic corridors. (Note: the yonic imagery does not contribute specifically to the setting in its own right but plays on the themes of sexual assault in the film). The Nostromo took science fiction and grounded it in the world of the everyday, the crew no longer made up of scientists but average working joes.

In doing so, *Alien* took those elements that would later make the summer camps of slasher films so effective: isolation, confinement, and threat. In the depths of space, the only thing protecting you from a quick and sudden death is the metal between you and the void and there is no one coming to help.

Alien is just one example. To find another we can look closer to home. *Evil Dead* alumni Scott Spiegel wrote and directed *Intruder* (1989) a slasher film (with excessively gory deaths) that was entirely set in a supermarket during the nightly stocking of the shelves. *Hellbound: Hellraiser II* (1988) begins with a hospital and an insane asylum but progresses into the depths of hell itself. In a similar fashion, *As Above, So Below* places its story in the catacombs of Paris and finds its way into hell itself. *The Pyramid* (2014) uses found footage to explore the inside of an Egyptian pyramid. Later we'll even explore a setting that is the inside of a serial killer's mind. All of these settings are able to leverage themselves as effective sites/sights for terror.

But horror can also be quite expansive, location wise. Both versions of *Dawn of the Dead* (1978, 2004) use an entire mall as a setting. *The Crazies* (2010) has its violence and terror spill out across the streets of a small town, USA. *Deliverance* takes the backwoods setting of horror but keeps it fresh with the raging river and white water rafting. *The Houses that October Built* (2014) is a road trip horror film that uses real haunted house attractions across the United States. *The Wicker Man* (1973) and *Apostle* (2018) both use the entirety of the islands that they are set on. Horror, in stark contrast to what many think, does not need to limit itself in geographical scope; there are no spatial constraints to horror. It depends on how you use it.

A new twist on a familiar location isn't as easy as it may seem and perhaps you're not up to the task of reinventing the wheel. In that case, what about a location that hasn't been used or one whose potential has only barely been explored?

Death Spa (1989) and *Killer Workout* (1987) have already claimed the gym as a slasher film location but what about a slasher set in a hardware store? Or what about a haunted sports stadium? Maybe you mix and match a little. We've all seen hospitals in horror but there's so much to hospitals beyond just hallways and patients' beds: What about an exorcism performed in the operation theater? What about an exorcism on a tall ship? Or a slasher on a blimp? With a little bit of creativity, the horror genre has a bunch of untapped settings that would make for a hell of a ride. You just gotta find them.

Psychological Baggage and Places of Disempowerment

One of the points I've stressed throughout the book is the idea of thinking about the audience member and the psychological processes that they experience when watching a movie. Setting plays a powerful, powerful role in these psychological processes and we will be exploring particular elements of setting shortly. First, let's take a look at the concept of psychological baggage and then explore how this affects what I call **Places of Disempowerment**.

When we as audience members see a location, we bring to it all of our personal psychological baggage. Funeral homes remind us of death, hospitals remind us of sick loved ones or of being sick ourselves. Psychological baggage is another reason that certain locations show up again and again with horror. This psychological baggage is brought in by the audience simply by using the setting—this means that even the most basic depiction of a funeral home will trigger thoughts related to them. However, that baggage works against you if the audience isn't enjoying the film and so it's important to explore new ways of twisting the locations.

Many of the locations that carry psychological baggage are also places of disempowerment. These are locations that make a person feel small, weak, frail; in a word: disempowered. The woods are great fun with friends but terrifying when you find yourself alone at night, trapped and lost in the dark you suddenly feel quite small. Being trapped in the depths of space with nowhere to run?

Stuck in an asylum? Hospital? Jail? School? Locations that disempower your characters work to disempower the audience through the mirroring effect we discussed above. But unlike the characters in our films, these locations are real. It might not be Silent Hill Hospital, but they've been to a hospital. They bring psychological baggage with them from their own experiences in such places of disempowerment.

But these locations don't always even need to be where the horror comes from. Think about *Hereditary* (2018). One of the most powerfully emotional moments in a film that's full of them is when Toni Collette goes to grief counseling and spills her guts. Not everyone has been to grief counseling but as emotional apes we are able to partake in the experience with an understanding of the emotional cocktail being presented. But a scene like that has an entirely different set of psychological baggage to it.

Another wonderful example of this is *Starry Eyes*, a film in which we follow a struggling actress chasing after her big break.

It takes her to the depths of Hollywood hell in a way that is entirely poignant on a rewatch following the #MeToo movement. Sexual misconduct is rampant in Hollywood and *Starry Eyes* shows us a worst case scenario version of such misconduct. For the perfect example of a place of disempowerment just look at any of the interviews that Sarah gives. These interviews move forward the plot—where *Hereditary*'s served to build character.

Both of these films show that a place of disempowerment doesn't merely have to be a place with psychological baggage but a place of disempowerment can also be location-as-situation. A grief meeting and a job interview are both events but they are events that take place as locations into themselves.

Location and Character

Some places just have a feeling, there's something about the way they are used in film that leaves them feeling like a character in the same way the actors do. This isn't unique to location, objects can also function as characters in their own right: The briefcase in *Pulp Fiction* (1994) or the car in *Low Blow* (1986). These objects have ascended the realm of the ordinary, they are as imbued with life as the furniture in *Beauty and the Beast* (1991). Not every setting needs to play with character; sometimes a house is just a house, a grief meeting just a grief meeting. Not every possible element belongs in every script but if you're looking for a way to craft a memorable location, even if it's one that's been done a hundred times, then perhaps it's time to explore the ways your setting and your characters interact.

The most obvious example of **Location is Character** is Tarsem Singh's *The Cell* (2000). A deranged serial killer falls into a coma before the police can discover where he's keeping his last victim, we only see that she's somewhere and trapped in a glass box that's slowly filling with water. It's up to a child psychologist with a new technology that allows her to enter into comatose patients' minds to save her. She plugs into the mind of the serial killer and we are treated to one of the most bizarre landscapes ever put to film.

From gorgeous palaces to the sewers formed out of non-euclidean shapes, rooms flow from one another like in a dream. But the dream isn't just a nightmare, it's the nightmare of a very, very sick mind and we're not just exploring his twisted psychology here: we are taking a Sunday stroll right through it. While *The Cell* might be the most direct version of this, there are other films that touch on dreamscapes to represent a part of psychology. One of the best examples in film history is the German Expressionist movement of film and *Das Cabinet des Dr. Caligari* (*The Cabinet of Dr. Caligari*, 1920).

The German Expressionist movement often rejected a naturalistic approach to setting and instead focused on blurred objects, odd angles, sharp edges, and distorted figures. This allowed for the sets to serve as reflections of the subjective emotions of the characters and how they viewed the world they were stuck in. *Caligari* takes this a step further than the rest. We open on a lovely, yet decidedly cold garden where we meet protagonist Francis who proceeds to tell an old man the twisted tale of how he and his fiance have come to be there. The story introduces a village made up of impossible angles, a madman, a murderer, and a flight across the jagged rooftops.

From the setting, to the way that it's dressed in shadows, every element feeds into the emotional experience we are hearing about. But it's not until the end that we come to learn that the wicked Dr. Caligari is actually just the director of the asylum in which Francis is a patient. The world that we were seeing is colored by the subjective perspective of an insane man and all of its impossibilities come out of the land of fantasy and into the land of psychoanalysis.

The Cabinet of Dr. Caligari is another example, like *The Cell*, that really elevates the idea of Location is Character. However, every time Freddy Krueger sneaks into the dreams of his victims, every time a character has a nightmare about some event in their life, (almost) every time someone gets drugged in a Cronenbergian way, the chance to explore the setting of the dream/experience is pushed front and center and can serve to offer a geographical insight into the psychology of your characters.

Then there are those places that aren't merely reflections of characters but are characters themselves. I call these **Location as Character**. Both *The Cell* and *Dr. Caligari* would fit into this category as well because the locations that they created are so unique and so impactful to the story that they truly feel like places of their own. However, because they are just absolutely so reflective of their character's psychologies, they fit best as under Location is Character. Location as Character settings are those that seem to have a life of their own—not because they are haunted but because they so deeply influence the story in tone and atmosphere.

The Shining will never get enough love from me and so how could I give up the opportunity to mention The Overlook Hotel? The Overlook is made up of endless twists and turns, open spaces and tight corridors, captured in tracking shots that disorient the audience, windows where there shouldn't—couldn't—be any. The Overlook is a place that makes no sense, where people never leave and where Jack Torrance has always been the caretaker. The Overlook is Unknowable Evil in the same fashion as Michael Myers, The Overlook is a psychopath that you pray you can escape but it closes you off, keeps you stuck with storms, tries to disorient you and trap you inside of itself. We'll be talking about the threat that locations offer in a moment and some of those locations are characters but none of them screams as loudly as The Overlook. The

Overlook doesn't need to hurt you, The Overlook is the dark voice whispering in your ear that you should kill your family.

But we don't need to keep our sights as limited as The Overlook or *The House of Usher* (1960). These are two locations that exist as little bubbles upon themselves that shield them from the world at large. David Lynch's *Blue Velvet* (1986) introduces Lumberton, North Carolina, a small town with some big secrets and a very dark side. Lynch is a master of building unique locations, look no further than the delightful *Twin Peaks*, but in *Blue Velvet* Lynch isn't exploring a town—*Blue Velvet* is a neo-noir thriller (that is as scary as any horror film) which focuses on amateur detective work, the criminal underground, and a kidnapped child.

As seen through the eyes of Lynch, the town of Lumberton, North Carolina, is a perfect slice of Americana; it's everything people mean when they say "the good ol' days." From torch singers in a neon bathed club to the girl next door, the affable police detective, the family run business and the dinner you go to grab milkshakes, *Blue Velvet* takes painstaking steps to ensure that you feel Lumberton as that fabled land where the American dream still lives and breathes.

But like any good character, Lumberton has its secrets and its own kind of darkness. Under its peaceful veneer this cozy little town hides the rotting flesh of a criminal underworld that threatens to infect everything around it. We're introduced to this underworld throughout the course of the investigation into the kidnapped child that, an investigation sparked by the chance discovery of a served human ear; as the plot develops, we see more of the location which ties it closely to the plot. But I don't want you to miss the forest for the trees. Character arcs develop alongside and through plot; in the same way, the character of location can't help but develop out of plot as well.

We are given foreshadowing of the developments to come through the opening sequence: a child at play, a waving firefighter, an afternoon cup of tea, a man taking care of his lawn, a heart attack—this is a place that holds pain as well as purity. But then the camera pushes into the grass until the screen is nothing more than the limbs and contortions of the insects under the surface, just out of sight but there if you look. There is as much depth to Lumberton as there is to Mima in *Perfect Blue* (1997) or Anna in *Possession* (1981).

When designing locations, we can take the time to think about how they feed into our stories and into our characters. With a little bit of thought, even our locations can be seen as characters like The Overlook Hotel, the always raining New York City of *Se7en*, the picture perfect Lumberton with its dark secrets, or the reflection of poverty and teenage emotional confusion that seeps from the setting of *It Follows*.

Location as Threat and Places of Infection

We're entering the section of the chapter that could be labelled "Location Driving the Plot." Except for the discussion on locational mood that closes out this chapter, the next several sections deal with locations that have a heavy weight to them and touches on isolation, sieges, confinement and, of course, threat. It is without a doubt that a location under siege is a location that is threatened but **Location as Threat** refers not to an outside or psychological trigger. Here we'll be looking at those locations that are the villains in and of themselves.

The most obvious example of location as threat comes from the long history of haunted houses that populate our horror tales. It can be argued that the first cinematic haunted house was *Le Manoir du Diable* (*The Haunted Castle*, 1896), an early Georges Méliès short that many (including myself) place as the first horror movie ever made. However, *The Haunted Castle* is not so much haunted as it is assailed by Mephistopheles—the short begins with a bat flying into the castle and turning into the big M himself. Therefore, the threat is not the location and, in fact, the location actually provides the tool (a cross) that the hero needs to repel the fiend. However, there are many haunted habitations that channel their danger through the location rather than just feature a threat within the location.

The Grudge is a 2004 remake of the Japanese ghost story *Ju-on: The Grudge* (2002). It concerns the vengeful spirits of a wrongfully murdered mother and son, offering plenty of spine-chilling moments of supernatural horror that propelled the remake to a box office of nearly $190 million. The primary threat in the film is the vengeful spirits but they are connected directly to the house, in a very interesting way. One problem that every haunted house story needs to overcome is the question of "Why the hell don't the protagonists get out of there?" *The Grudge* answers this question by positioning the house not as what confines the ghosts but as a liminal space that stands between the safety of ordinary reality and the world of supernatural curses.

When one crosses over the threshold of the Saeki house they expose themselves to the curse, the grudge, of the murdered family and are doomed to die at their hands. Merely taking a step into the house threatens your life. Where the Saeki house is a threat because it leads to a curse, the titular room *1408* (2007) offers a different approach to location as threat. Mike Enslin is a skeptic of the paranormal that writes the kind of ghost story–haunted attraction books you see in line at the grocery store. Pointed towards room 1408 at the Dolphin hotel, Mike takes the room regardless of the hotel manager's attempts to dissuade him. Mike enters 1408 and descends into his own personalized hell.

The ghosts of past victims begin to scare him, the window slams shut on him, the sprinklers cut off communication, the door won't open, reality bends and twists and wraps and Mike experiences his worst emotional fears, relives his past trauma and struggles to prevent any new trauma. The rules of time and space, action and reaction bottoms out and the realm of the psychological fuses with the paranormal in a room versus man acid trip of an encounter. Room 1408 functions like a pocket dimension to hell stuffed inside a luxury hotel. The threat is not from the ghosts that remain but from the psychological toll the room takes on those that enter—it wants to to make you kill yourself.

Some places are just evil, tucked away on an innocent street in Japan or kept hush-hush and hidden by hotel staff. These places have to be ventured to, they are self-contained spaces. It's terrifying to be stuck at sea and realize that you're on the *Death Ship* (1980), a vessel that will attack you with every hook, rope, and piece of gear it has lying around. But there are spaces out there from which infection leaks and it changes what surrounds it. The *Event Horizon* traveled through a hell dimension and brought it to our reality, the ship (as a location) threatens the entire universe. *Aterrados* (*Terrified*, 2017) charts a paranormal infestation as it infects a whole neighbourhood. But let's look at how two horror legends handled **Places of Infection**: John Carpenter and Stephen King.

We've already looked at how John Carpenter's *Prince of Darkness* challenges ideological beliefs to generate a feeling of abjection from the audience but it is a fantastic example of a place of infection and highlights the kinds of ramifications that Scream Writers should keep in mind while exploring their own places of infection. The locus of the infection is the basement of an abandoned Los Angeles church that has been hiding a powerful secret. Lucifer himself is trapped as a sentient liquid, ready to be released back upon the world; the only way to stop him from corrupting and returning to his place as ruler of reality is by deciphering a scientifically encoded book left by the alien Jesus who had trapped Lucifer. As the time grows nearer, the powers of Lucifer grow but he is trapped in his liquid form, nearly immobile. But the threat of Lucifer is looked at as a presence, an infection of the area.

It begins with the homeless people in the streets around the church. They have given into Lucifer's control, submitted to his will. We'll see this explored in a similar fashion when we turn to *It*. Both *Prince of Darkness* and *It* feature creatures or entities corrupting the setting, they twist and contort the areas around them and change the fundamental social structures of the area they are in. Sometimes the location and the threat within can be so powerful as to completely control the way of life surrounding it, such as in *The Shrine* or *The Ruins* where the locals will not hesitate to kill those that threaten the semblance of peace they have found in the shadow of power.

Prince of Darkness shows us the beginning of a corruption, how it spreads to those that are desperate and hungry, the forgotten. An infection grows if you don't cut it off at the head, until over time the society is destroyed or adapts. *Prince of Darkness* cut the infection off at the arm. The same can't be said about Derry, Maine and Stephen King's *It*.

Pennywise the Dancing Clown feeds on children and their fear. This shapeshifting creature returns every 27 years to claim its victims but, much like the great Cthulhu, its slumber can be felt by those close to it. When talking about a Stephen King work, one has to pare away the tapestry of evil that is King's Maine. The world that Stephen King writes about is one which is interconnected and has grown through additions across a career spanning decades. But looking at *It* alone, one feels the seething anger and fear that Pennywise instills: violence is ignored, racism, child abuse … nothing matters, there is a blind eye of ignorance, a malevolent force that seeps throughout the town from the sewers.

The town feels like an enemy, something the remake captured amazingly well by layering Pennywise the clown into graffiti and the backgrounds of public places. No one can be trusted, our protagonists are on their own—the town's obsession is able to reflect the characters psychological journeys much in the same way the setting of *It Follows* reflects the feelings of isolation surrounding teenage sexual awakening and experiencing poverty. Unlike *It Follows*, no one will help you in Derry—no one would react if your father beat you to death or if the bully's left you covered in scars. Derry is a benign tumor—the infection is contained but it is no longer a part of us—of mankind.

Places of Isolation and Confinement

Isolation and confinement, the two go hand in hand often but not always. One can be stuck with friends and therefore not isolated, likewise you can be isolated but not confined—except, of course, to your body—like in the famous *Twilight Zone* episode, *Time Enough at Last* (1959). Isolation and confinement can be the main feature of a story, such as in *The Descent*, or merely a moment of the greater whole like when Laurie is stuck in the closet in *Halloween*. Places of isolation and confinement are charged places, they arise out of the emotional energy that is invested into them—if a character is okay with being trapped underground, *The Descent* isn't nearly as scary.

Likewise, Laurie could spend hours in that closet without any problems if it was just a normal day in her life. What's worse for Laurie, she's trapped inside a place of isolation and confinement that is itself trapped within a larger place of isolation and confinement, the house. Because any location can serve as a place of isolation and confinement, it's important to understand what the emotional experiences of isolation and confinement do to the human brain.

Isolation and confinement both serve as triggers of emotional behaviour. When we feel isolated, we feel as if we are trapped within ourselves and there are numerous negative effects on psychological health. While the majority of negative effects are seen as a result of long term isolation, these effects are often accelerated in cinema due to the heavy psychological and emotional weight of the events that make up a horror film. It's important to note that character and plot can work to create places of isolation within large groups of people: the loner at school, people are there but the location is now a site of isolation. However, this isolation is one that is beaten at the end of every day when the bell rings. Because of this, the long term effects are less likely to be a problem. This is where we look to confinement.

Places of containment are cut off from the outside world. This could be achieved with summer camps, like we saw earlier. But this could also be the work of a plot agent turning a location into one of containment. Take the school example about isolation: the outside world gets cut off (zombie outbreak, paranormal shenanigans, psychopathic madman, take your pick) and turns the school into a place of containment. Now the feelings of isolation are going to increase for our loner because there is no longer that light at the end of the tunnel.

Instead, tensions will rise and the psychological toll being paid by the emotional mind is so great that negativity easily slips in and magnifies the situation. We saw this happen with *The Mist* when the supermarket became a place of containment and it was used to fuel the rest of the film. Containment is such a powerful source of negative energy; the super-ego that contains the id is overwhelmed and the societal structures governing "proper" behavior begin to fade away. Being in a place of containment means that there is no more law except for the survival of the fittest.

Slashers, zombie outbreaks, infections, hauntings. Containment immediately increases the stakes involved in any horror situation and so it is one of the most commonly used elements within horror. However, places of containment don't have to dominate a story. The most famous moment of *28 Days Later* (2002) is the spectacle of empty London streets. The film sets its scope quite large as we travel out of the empty city and along the roads leading away. But the third act is within a place of confinement the protagonists are trapped in.

When isolation and confinement work together, their negative energies—the way they work on the animal parts of the brain, survival, sex, aggression, fear—often feed into each other. Returning to *The Mist*, this cycle is elegantly demonstrated through the growing cult. This is because despite being a monster movie, *The Mist* is ultimately using the monsters as a backdrop for exploring how humans cope with isolation and confinement: Isolation and confinement, us against them, that special cocktail that makes the dumb jock in every slasher movie somehow even more aggressive.

Perhaps the most common examples of isolation and confinement within modern horror come from the zombie genre. A house, mall, or military base, all become places of confinement and isolation when under attack.

Locations Under Siege aren't much different than typical confinement and isolation; except for the fact there is something that wants to get in and kill you and you have nowhere to flee. And, depending on what is laying siege, you may be on your feet all night, day, week, whatever, because it has intelligence like the goons in *Assault on Precinct 13* (1976) or *Dog Soldiers* (2002).

Or, you could be safe but confined in an isolated location having to listen to the moans of the walking dead, a constant reminder just in case you thought you could find a moment of relaxation. Being stuck in the middle of a snow lift like in *Frozen* (2010) is one kind of confinement, it's another when it's a living, or unliving, entity out there that wants to get you. A location under siege takes all of the pressures of places of confinement, and isolation, and injects them with a shot of adrenalin like Uma Thurman in *Pulp Fiction*. People crack, bad decisions get made and tension generated in the characters is surfused throughout the audience.

Locational Mood

So far we have looked at locations in an abstract form, examining the cognitive responses related to them and how they can be used to isolate, threaten, or produce a feeling of fragility and powerlessness. In order to produce these reactions we looked at the emotional baggage a location can hold, how locations can make us feel small, and how isolation and confinement can negatively influence the emotional field of our characters. These elements can be reshuffled, reused, and rearranged in a plethora of ways across our stories or even within a singular story. However, these elements are abstractions: Yes, this story is set in a place of isolation and confinement but that means nothing in and of itself—the location itself still remains a haunted house, a supermarket, a high school, et. al.

Let us not lose sight of the importance of the physical location while we're exploring the psychological tools and ramifications that best allow us to provoke a reaction in the viewer. Because we are going to be looking at the physical space itself, it's important to make sure that we understand what is meant by **Mise-en-Scène**. First, mise-en-scène is not actually a production term, it is an academic term which refers to the arrangement of everything that appears in the frame: clothing, sets, actors, lighting, props, decor, etc. Mise-en-scène is then everything that we see—it is the outcome of the collaboration between the many people responsible to bring a movie to life.

However, this term is very important to our discussion; we are placing ourselves, intellectually and creatively, in the world that we are creating—we are entering the physical space of our characters and are able to control, to a degree, what elements should be present in the mise-en-scène. We saw an example of this when we explored how Bill Lancaster used his screenplay to control the lighting of the dog kennel scene in *The Thing*. But lighting is only one small aspect of the whole that is mise-en-scène. Where else do we control and what can we do with this control?

Let's begin with the space itself. We have complete control over the spaces that we represent within our writing: size, shape, location, age, style; all of the elements that combine to situate a location within temporal space are completely created through our generation of a location. Furthermore, there is no reason for the Scream Writer to feel trapped within the realms of reality or, rather, within their mental framework of reality. For example, the word hospital brings to mind a large building, many, many rooms, lots of activity, people coming and going all hours of the day. However, just because the hospitals that me or you have encountered mesh well with these descriptive terms doesn't mean that the hospital in our stories have to.

We can control the size, activity, and functions of the hospital we are creating. We could even, if we so choose, decide our version of a hospital is little bigger than a corner store. Because we have this control over the location, we are able to best design the location to mesh with our desired cognitive outcomes. We could place the hospital on a mountain to explore isolation and confinement, we could make it a sick ward, a threat, or a place of infection. Or, we could just have it be a regular hospital.

The level of control that we have is often forgotten because we have models of buildings and places within our minds that have been built up by our experiences, both physically being in a similar place or experiencing them within film, television and text. These mental models are fantastic for understanding the essence of a location and for quickly sharing information and stories about them without needing to explain the concept of hospital every time you talk about one. But these mental models are so ingrained in our minds that we often forget that they are not representatives of a "divine" location but rather a combination of many different locations that we have encountered and used to build that model.

Our mental models exist within a temporal arrangement, as well. I say hospital, you think of a hospital. But if I said a 17th century hospital, your brain would quickly scan the information included in your mental model of a hospital and eliminate those elements that it deems to be irrelevant; this is done by running through what you know about the 17th century, hospitals of the 17th century, and hospitals today. You may not know very much about 17th century hospitals but a mental model would be built out of what you do know and what you can infer such as the level of technologies and medical science.

However, our mental models do not regularly scale down in the same manner. 'Hospital' could bring to mind decades of experiences within and seeing hospitals without separating the elements of each experience by their temporal happenings. One reason this happens is because of the two-systems in the brain. There is a fast system and a slow system. (Though, technically speaking, it is one system but this division, as explored by Daniel Kahneman, is for the purposes of clarity.) Our fast brain jumps into action quickly and accepts what appears to be correct.

Our slow system is activated when we have to think through problems and engage our minds actively; however, our slow system is lazy and is more than willing to accept the judgements of the faster system. So, our fast system brings to mind our mental model when we think of hospitals and our slower system accepts the temporal range of data because they are similar in appearance. Because of such, we have to be careful with following our mental models without thinking about what they are really representing for us.

So, we have control over what size, shape and age the space is. Let's move in tighter and explore the control we have over what is inside of that space and how it appears. The feeling of a location is a combination of lighting, objects, age, and mood. What do I mean by mood here? Mood is made through the combination of everything but it is also a part of the descriptive language used. A hospital room described as cold and sterile has a different feel than a hospital room that is warm and relaxing. The words that we choose to describe our locations are the most important part of contributing to the mood of the location.

However, lighting, objects, age, and the physical attributes of the location all combine to work in conjunction with mood—therefore, we could offset the feeling of that cold and sterile hospital room by including a pot of flowers and get well soon balloons; their inclusion would create a contrast within the room and we can play with that (perhaps we want to contrast the cold feeling of medical science with the hopes and wishes we place on it for the people inside those rooms). So, while descriptive language is our strongest way to influence mood, it's important that we don't rely exclusively on it.

The objects that we fill our houses with say a lot about us. When it comes to our belongings, many of us unknowingly extend our conceptualization of 'I' to include our belongings such as our house, car, or even prized objects (in my case, my collection of out of print film studies texts and my Bergman screenplays both fall into my conceptualization of myself). So, knowing this, how can we use it to our advantage? It's one thing for us, as living members of the dominant reality, to explore what we mean when we say 'I,' but what does it mean for our characters? First, it is not of extreme importance to identify which specific objects are a part of our characters conceptualizations. This is because film works differently than reality.

Everything we include within our screenplays has a reason, therefore every object within a character's home, to a degree, is reflectively of their inner psychology. The very fact of an object being mentioned gives it meaning: I, the writer, may have posters, decorations, or possessions that are not reflective of my psychology but have come into my possession through others or through temporary whims; but every object of our characters is reflective of their psychology and therefore makes use of the mise-en-scène to bring the audience closer to the character—this is why bad art direction can stand out so strongly in a film, it doesn't reflect the location or character and has a jarring effect. Second, the objects that we choose to include at the screenplay stage can be a powerful way of helping the director, cinematographer, actors, and all of those involved with decision making in the production process, to enter into the world of our stories and into the minds of the characters—it is a way of telegraphing aspects of our characters in a quick manner that could be the defining factor to understanding them.

But not every location is a reflection of a character. In horror, we often visit police stations, run down buildings, hospitals, libraries, schools, asylums, and many places that are within the control of a broader organization—often the government but not always—or outside of the domain of man (at least living man) such as the rundown and haunted castles, the deep dark woods, or even the open road of the highway. Let us first explore those locations controlled by a "higher power."

The government is a feature in all of our lives, regardless of our opinions on it. Even if we consider ourselves to be too cool to care, our rebel attitude first requires a government for us to rebel against; without it, our persona and attitude would not exist. At times the government is seen as a Big Brother figure; other times it's the benevolent force we need to protect us (such as our health care and police systems). Regardless of our opinions, it is important that we try to understand the values and goals of the government in regards to the locations we display within our stories. For example, let's say that we are writing about a possessed criminal that gets brought to jail. We realize that we want to have a detective fight for the criminal's soul while he's locked up, so we have the detective grab a crucifix off the wall.

Not what people think of as being in a police station but hey, ours is different and so it does. However, this raises questions about the separation of church and state and actually opens up our world in profound ways. And here we thought we were just making the story work. Maybe one of the cops is a Christian and that's why it's there? Building on our idea the space we call home, this would seem a logical connection to make. However, it's important that we realize that these locations are not the characters' homes. In fact, they do not belong to the characters at all.

When it comes to government controlled locations, the objects within are reflective of the government itself and what is permissible. This means that the requirements of the law are an important factor. That doesn't mean that we can't have a crucifix in a police station. But it does mean that our inclusion of it requires an examination of the world we have written. We need to ask ourselves why this is there when it shouldn't be and how that is reflective of the attitudes of those that run the station.

But, as we all know, the government moves slow, is often overworked, and underfunded. So, we can also explore ideas relating to the funding our locations have received. A police station lacking the necessary funds to fully equip themselves will carry with it a different feeling than one that looked like it came out of an episode of *CSI*. These changes are important for us to contemplate because they allow us to transform our mental models into living, breathing locations. But they bring about changes to the milieu that our stories exist within and if we are aware of these then we are able to fully bring our worlds to life. This doesn't mean we should transform our stories to be about these changes but if we work them into the background and the world then they will flesh out our locations and stories in a way that adds depth and reveals a deep level of immersion and forethought on the part of the Scream Writer.

Finally, looking at those locations that exist outside of personal or governmental control, we are faced with a problem. If our choices are not reflective of a character's psychology or an institution's protocols and laws, then how is it that we can change a forest into something more than just a grouping of trees? More than ever, our control of these interstitial locations comes from our control of mood, particularly those descriptive words that flavour our writing. A forest whose trees block out the sun has a different feel, and implied lighting, than a bright and cheery green thicket. However, where our previous locations ask for descriptive words of the objects inside, I recommend against picking the types of trees and greens in a forest as it is almost certainly going to be out of your ability to control where the production shoots.

When it comes to run down locations, haunted houses and the like, the objects picked may be reflective of a character (such as the previous, now ghostly, inhabitants) but more often than not the objects within are picked for their mood itself. These locations are almost always historical and the wear and tear of the ancient art and craftsmanship that went into their design and construction has grown over with cobwebs, stains, dust and the harshness of time.

This creates a contrast between the story, our present with the characters, and the location itself, and this gives a feeling of stepping out of time and observing an existence that is almost alien to us. This is heightened with our choice of mood words but is in itself one of the most powerful of mood setters; perhaps it's no surprise so many horrors happen in these older locations? Much like we see with serial killer films, horror arises out of the past to confront the present. We are afraid of facing our past, and in a world that has seen slavery, genocides, and the horrors of industrialization, perhaps we are right to fear it.

Understanding the power of mood and objects go a long way to shape our feelings about locations. When working in conjunction with isolation, confinement and the other elements we have explored this chapter, we are able to create memorable and terrifying locations that serve our stories' purposes and bring the audience deeper into our worlds. But these locations serve no purpose without a story to drive it. With that in mind, let's turn our attention towards that cruel mistress: the plot.

Exercises

1. List each of the locations in your screenplay. Write out one way that each adds dimension to the characters or the world.

2. Building off of the previous list, for each location write any emotional baggage the protagonists may have for that location and how being in it makes them feel.

3. How do your locations make use of isolation and confinement? What prevents your characters from leaving to find safety or authority?

4. How important is location to your Scream Play? If you moved the story halfway across the world would it make a difference? If so then explore ways you can connect the location to the characters and events of the story. When location is working in conjunction with character and theme, the world of the story is that much richer.

5. You have identified that your story deals with infection. What are the geographical logistics of your infection? Does it spread out in a wave like *Prince of Darkness* or is it more sporadic like the infectious parasite of *Splinter* (2008)?

Chapter 5: Plots

There are two different stories in horror: internal and external. In external horror films, the evil comes from the outside, the other tribe, this thing in the darkness that we don't understand. Internal is the human heart.

John Carpenter

Monsters, scares, and locations are useless on their own. Without a reason to be, they are nothing more than abstracts. Not that they are valueless, however. Perhaps contemplating a monster sparked an idea and you jotted down some notes for a possible scene. Already, you have turned to plot, which is simply the events that make up your story.

Any event is a part of the plot. The way that events are placed creates the structure of the story. There is an endless amount of ways we can structure our plots. We will explore some of the more popular structures, but I'll also share a couple of the oddball favorites that I've used for scripts in the past. But let us first turn our attention towards the grand forms that propel horror stories.

The Seven Struggles of Horror

Looking at the plots of stories from throughout history, Rudyard Kipling argued that there were only 69 plots in the world. Carlo Gozzi argued for 36. Ronald B. Tobias says 20. And lonely old Aristotle settled for two. Stories are malleable and so too is the definition of plot. Therefore, the **Seven Struggles of Horror** makes no claim to being perfected—the art form and our perception of it are too involved to allow for perfection. However, these seven factors are used to propel 90% of horror. As a story progresses, it may interact with several of these struggles as the narrative demands it.

The reason I have picked these seven key areas is because I believe that through them we can see a lot about the human condition and how they play on our fears to cover all the conceivable threats and traits that drove our evolutionary path.

Mystery

Mankind was never the strongest of animals. We lack the natural weapons given to the bear. Nor can we see into the darkness of the night like the panther. Or leave the ground like the owl or the hawk. Mankind's limitations should have stunted their growth, the natural predators thinning the herds. But we touched the monolith, so to speak.

Mankind's curiosity, coupled with (or perhaps even driven by) it's level III consciousness, has allowed humans to master tool use and the art of complex planning. It's easy for us to forget that lights and heating still count as technology in this techno-future world that is our reality, it's even easier to forget just how long it took mankind to rise to this position. The human, as we think of ourselves now in an anatomical sense, dates to over 300,000 years ago. They only began to move out of Africa about 50,000 years ago. To put this in perspective: Rome was founded 2,771 years ago and we refer to that as ancient history or the classics.

Behind every decision that we made—from where we sheltered at night, what was on the other side of the valley, what was edible, behind all of them—was the unknown, that illustrious and terrifying nothingness that is actually everything. The unknown leaves us so very uncomfortable but yet we know that is where progress is made. It is in the unknown that you find better hunt, better berries, better weather. The unknown is a risk but it is a risk that has rewarded our evolution and progress, whether it's the unknown of the physical world around us, the scientific, or the spiritual. We chase after the rewards of mystery. But where there are rewards, there are dangers. There are larger predators, poisonous berries, worse weather. There are also atom bombs and Manson families. The unknown remains terrifying for this reason but we're a species of gamblers.

The mystery, that piece of the unknown that we may just be able to unravel (for better or worse) is the first of our struggles because it is the oldest. However, it is one of the oddest in that within itself there is no horror. Mystery for the sake of mystery might be fulfilling but when it comes to the horror genre, it must reveal that the threat is real (or, rather, the protagonist is led to believe it is real). *The Fly* (1986), *The Blair Witch Project*, *Antichrist* (2009), all begin with a mystery: Is teleportation possible? Is the Blair Witch real? Can I treat my wife? But they turn into transformation, response, survival. Perhaps the closest film to being a pure mystery horror film is *The Wicker Man*, though it proves itself to have been an escape film in disguise in its titular scene.

The unknown might be our greatest fear but we're always interested to know what's really there. Is it something that will help me? Is it something that wants to eat me? To trap me? Use me? Change me? Drive me insane?

Survival

A middle-aged salesman takes his Plymouth Valiant out on the open road. It's a business trip but that doesn't mean he can't enjoy himself, take in the California canyons that the two lane highway bisects. What should be a fun and easy trip becomes a fight for survival when the driver of a Peterbilt 281 takes offense at being passed. With size on his side, the truck could easily run our salesman off the road but instead he decides to play with him, to taunt him, tease him, and drive him to his wits end. How does it play out? You'll have to watch Spielberg's *Duel* (1971) and find out for yourself. It is a film that boils the theme of survival down into its most pure form: Man against.

Turning the clock back a couple hundred thousand years, we again find the root of this struggle in the experiences of pre-linguistic man. Man against animal, the fight to survive and carve out our own niche in the world. Perhaps we forget just how hard hunting truly was; we're so used to being angered at big game hunters standing over the carcasses of the deadliest hunters the natural world has ever seen—but try, if you might, to imagine what that struggle was like when our weapons were made of sticks and stones. The thrill of the modern hurt pales in comparison.

Often, as we see from cave paintings, the hunt involved groups of men armed and working together to bring down their prey. But what of those caught by surprise while gathering or scouting the land? What about the beasts that stalked at night, the screams of your tribal members fading into silence as they are carried from their home?

And let us not forget about the horrors that man inflicts on its own. In *The Better Angels of Our Nature: Why*

Violence has Declined, author Steven Pinker explores the history of violence from prehistoric man through our histories of wars, murders, lynchings, and all manner of grisly assaults. Pinker first introduces the readers to Ötzi, our oldest European mummy from the Chalcolithic period. Originally thought to have fallen while traversing the Tyrolean Alps and frozen to death, it was revealed that in fact Ötzi had an arrowhead embedded in his shoulder. Ötzi was not the victim of accident—he was murdered.

It was man that killed Ötzi. Animals were not the only threat to our ancestors. In fact, Pinker identifies that the logic behind violence shows the multitude of ways that we justify committing it against our own kind. We commit violence to take what we want from others: their supplies and their women. We kill out of fear: I'm worried that my neighbour might try to kill me so I strike first to get the advantage. Indeed, violence was such a normal part of everyday life that we see it "civilized" as we approach the modern age—while historically the lower classes were positioned as violent, respectable gentlemen didn't hesitate to take up arms to defend their honor in a duel.

And lest we forget that monster of the modern age: The serial killer, those humans that kill for reasons unfathomable. We may have identified serial killing as a behaviour in the 20th century but it's roots are surely deep in the soil of history. As far back as 331 BC we have reports of a series of poisonings (at first believed to be a plague) that was traced to two women, of which Livy claimed their actions were the result of madness rather than felonious intent.

The flip side of the coin that is our historical violence is our drive for survival. We do not die easily, look no further than Rasputin or Payton Leutner for proof of that. We fight to survive with every fibre of our being, our genes demanding it of us so that they can live on, propagate, and experience the full breadth of human history—long after we ourselves are gone, our genes live on. The struggle of man against man, beast and nature is the struggle to control the planet, to be the top of the food chain. We've won; completely against beasts and, despite the rising fears of our times, we are currently killing each other less than we ever have before on a century by century basis. But that fear is still there, it's primal, part of our DNA, so we find ourselves exploring this age old struggle time and time again within horror.

Films about survival situate the threat as a physical entity that exists within the world and is separate from the protagonist. The entity wants to violently harm the protagonist. In films about survival the protagonist's primary goal is to survive in any way possible and they are not physically restricted by the entity. A perfect example is the films of the slasher genre. There is something that is trying to kill the characters, it might catch them off guard but they are not restricted by the entity. They might hole up in a closet but they put themselves there rather than climbing out a window.

Slasher films also help to highlight how these struggles interact with each other. Slasher films often have a whodunit element to them and thus cross survival with mystery. Is Harry Warden back from the dead in *My Bloody Valentine* (1981)? Just exactly who knows what they did last summer? But these elements are often relegated to a point of non-importance by their focus on killer vs teens. But moments of mystery arise within the films naturally such as the "where is everyone" searches that transition to the third acts of *Halloween* and *Friday the 13th.*

Survival also takes on elements of the escape film as well, such as the capturing of Sally and her subsequent tying to the table in *The Texas Chainsaw Massacre.* While an extended moment within the film, it isn't the goal of the movie but an escalation of the threat. Because both survival and escape require a hostile, physical other, they can be blended into a particularly nasty half and half. *Downrange* (2017) could be seen as a survival or an escape film: they are trying to survive a psychopathic sharpshooter but he has also pinned down, trapped, behind cover. They have freedom of mobility but he has a long range weapon.

The escalation of the film shows it to be primarily concerned with survival—the victory in the film is not the ability to flee and live but the explicit death of the psychopath—rather than escape and it ends with a minor moment of menace when one of our characters is able to turn the tables on the killer. Likewise, a zombie film can take its primary focus as survival, escape, or transformation: it depends on its focus.

Survival is the most used of the seven struggles, except for mystery, because it connects us with the most basic of our psychological mechanisms: fight or flight. We have the option to do both and what we choose determines our fate. Told by a deft hand, the survival film can be the most terrifying of experiences—in the horror film: a killer in the woods, a home invasion, a monster on the loose; in history: the threat of the other, tribal raiding and natural predators. The survival film may be derided as providing simple scares but a more useful framing would identify them as universal fears.

Escape

None of us want to be kidnapped. For one, we are social creatures and hate to be cut off. We also believe, or at least agree to approach reality as if we have free will. To be kidnapped means to have that violently taken from us. But it also means there's a reason. It might be to kill us. It might be to torture us. Sexually abuse us.

Or, if we're lucky, maybe they just want to take something of ours and this is the easiest way to do that. But, even the luckiest option still means a loss for us. If you are taking something of mine then I am in danger of you taking something that makes up my representation of "I." At the moment of writing this, I'm not in very much danger of that happening because the things that are a part of me are of sentimental value rather than monetary. That is a luxury I have in the 21st century.

However, we weren't always so lucky.

The dark of night is thick. The day was long, the hunt was good. Bellies are full and eyelids are heavy. There is food for now. There will be another hunt soon but they've been getting further between with the colder weather.

Shadows come in the night, beating the men into submission, slaughtering the young, snatching the women and the food. We see our fear of losing our stuff, as men. But the story of the woman is often left between the cracks. Seeing that experience speaks to half of the world's population and is our genetic birthright as a species, it's easy to see how the thoughts of kidnapping (even when for money) evoke a heavily sadistic and sexual undercurrent.

Escape might evoke survival but the primary focus is on the restriction of movement and regaining that freedom through the use of wits and willpower. These films may feature a conscious antagonist such as *10 Cloverfield Lane* (2016) and *Hounds of Love* (2016), in which case the films flirt with survival. However, the environment can also be the antagonist and comes in both conscious and unconscious forms such as the sharks in *Open Water* (2003) or the cold in *Frozen* or even getting lost in the woods like *The Blair Witch Project* (which blurs elements of escape, disaster, and madness). The primary element of escape is the restriction or containment of the protagonist against their will (or through unlucky circumstances). The object may be to survive but often the goal is freedom itself: *death on my terms, not yours.* In this way a downbeat ending as seen in *The Ruins* (2008) is still a victory, if only a pyrrhic one.

Stories of escape are about feeling helpless, trapped, incapable of overcoming the odds facing you but having to find a way despite the fact. Often films dealing with home invasion become films of escape. *Funny Games*, *The Collector* (2009), *Strangers*, and *À l'intérieur* (*Inside*, 2007) are films of escape that share elements of survival. They present people with limited means to fight back but that are overwhelmed and geographically cut off from help. If the character could only get out, get into the wide world out there, they would be safe. There is an arena inside which a battle of survival may take place but the goal remains escape and rejoining the world in which social obligations are once again observed and you are guaranteed your safety and freedom.

Films of madness tie in well with stories of escape, often the escape being from the protagonist's mind itself (though not always). *Rosemary's Baby* is a story of madness and transformation that demonstrates the inability of 1960s women to escape their husbands and the patriarchal system—it manages to set the elements of escape in a busy city in broad daylight, a feat which was possible through the borrowing of escape elements while having its primary focus elsewhere. *Rosemary's Baby* is one of a number of films that show society itself as being an inescapable beast, though this is most often done through contrasting urban dwellers with rural settings.

Eden Lake (2008) follows an urban couple that takes a romantic vacation to a lake hidden in the woods of the English countryside. They come into a battle of survival against a gang of youth that constantly leave our couple stuck, hiding or tied up and tortured. The focus of the film is clearly on escape, each scene building its tension of whether they will be able to get away or not. When Kelly Reilly, playing our lead Jenny, is finally able to escape from the woods she stumbles into a party held at a nearby house and they take her to the bathroom to get her cleaned up.

It turns out the house belongs to the parents of Brett, the sadistic leader of the youths, who convinces the party that Jenny and her boyfriend murdered the kids. Jenny screams as the door to the washroom is kicked down and the angry mob enters, the door closing behind them. This theme of thinking you have escaped only to encounter the larger truth of societal violence is shared by films such as *House of a 1000 Corpses* (2003) and *The Texas Chainsaw Massacre* remake from 2003. We experience the release of safety, only to be faced with the nihilism of the machine we are all trapped in.

Escape may come in the form of a struggle of the flesh but ultimately it is about a battle of the mind and regaining our sense of safety and belonging in the world. It can be a thrill, as certain BDSM communities attest to, but it is one of our primal fears that we use horror and roleplay to tap into. Our bodies are not in danger by either, but the mind returns to those old connections, those old emotions. We want to feel safe, we want to feel protected and we want to feel as if we are in control of our realities, our fates. But we are obsessed with stories about kidnappings, abductions, break ins, serial murderers, torture—both in our fiction and in our 24/7 news cycle. We want to feel helpless, if only vicariously.

Disaster

We can struggle to survive, fight off our attacker like the final girl of a slasher movie. We can escape, if we are lucky, and regain our freedom and become part of the larger social body again. Survival and escape put us to the test against another. This is rarely the case in struggles of disaster or, another way of framing them, stories of reaction. The struggle of disaster is focused on reacting to events that are beyond our control. We know from escape that our sense of self is important to our sense of wellbeing, as well as our sense of belonging to the larger social community.

Our sense of belonging socially is one of the three pillars of our psychological health. Also is the feeling that our actions control outcomes, that we are capable of exerting our physical and mental willpower to control our conscious experience by shaping the world around us. Disasters show us the dark side of humanity, when faced with threats they can't control, as well as the failings of the social order to protect the individual—in this way, disaster reinforces the ideas of *Eden Lake* and *Rosemary's Baby*: society itself may be the beast and its violence urges are brought to the surface in the face of disaster.

But disaster is more than just the collapse of social structures, it is also something that we crave and fear in equal parts. We're terrified of the end of the world and constantly think it's coming any moment: Y2K, 2012, North Korea, the 2012 Election, et. al. Our narratives of zombie and post-apocalypse worlds show that we position ourselves as the survivors of these disasters. Where does this fear come from? Why is it also laced with a power fantasy? What good could disaster have ever brought? Surely we would want to avoid disasters at any cost, right?

Well, perhaps not.

Let's return to our ancestor who was robbed in our escape example. We'll call him Bob. Bob has survived hunts-turned-massacres and enemy raids, although he lost his mate and his supplies. His has been a difficult existence but Bob believes in the tribe and their ability to bounce back, find some more prey and really thrive again. But the game is weak, the weather has been turning colder and the berries aren't as plentiful as they once were. As the snow starts, the tribe has to move. The cold kills, there's nothing to be done against it and the journey will kill the weaker members, perhaps even some of the stronger bodies, too. The world itself has risen up against Bob and his tribe, it is an absolute disaster.

With our mythic roots and stories of monsters and gods, perhaps the old kaiju of mankind are but the patterns of the weather. Cyclones, tsunamis, twisters, blizzards, droughts, thunder and lightning, volcanoes … all are all natural disasters that completely shift the social dynamic. Under stress, the weak will get left behind, people will fend for themselves, horde supplies and steal what they can get their hands on, maybe even club you to death to get to it. It is sheer chaos, the social order ruptured and stitched together out of our psychological neuroses. It's easy to see how terrifying a disaster is; in this modern day, many have survived through such frightening events. But what is to be gained here? Why do we look to it as a source of fantasy?

Let's catch back up with Bob. Bob survived the great migration to warmer lands, something that can't be said about many of the tribe. But Bob did and now his personal wealth, if he has it, or his shared wealth, through the tribe now having fewer divisors when it comes to resources. So, biologically speaking, the thinning of the herd allows the survivors an abundance of supplies. Now, of course, this is not always guaranteed: Bob is merely lucky to have survived, he wasn't fated to.

But Bob represents the figure through which we view ourselves within our fantasies: we are the survivors. Our brains weren't designed for the modern world, we work better in smaller groups; the thinning of the herd brings us back down to more psychologically manageable numbers of social connections. Less people means the brave and egotistical are more likely to make a name for themselves. Films of disaster give us the chance to be a victim or to be Bob.

Disasters come in all shapes and sizes. Disaster can be intimate such as in *Frozen* or *Open Water*, films that explore what happens when the individual faces a disaster in insolation, away from civilization's helping hand. Or disasters can come roaring in from the sea like in *Cloverfield* (2008) or *Shin Godzilla* (2016), beasts that represent nuclear annihilation or the power of natural disasters channeled into a physical entity. Intimate disasters remove the protagonists from society, highlighting the difficulty of the individual's struggle against nature when society is unable to intervene.

These films remind us that society is not always to be counted upon, that survival in the face of disaster rests on the individual. *Cloverfield* shows that the society which is supposed to protect us can fail miserably, those in charge unable to face the odds of nature in the end. However, it's not always bleak. *Shin Godzilla* focuses less on city destroying action than it does the political nature of dealing with a disaster. The threat here is not just Godzilla but a possible nuclear strike by Russian or American forces on Japanese soil: a wound that no one wants to reopen. *Shin Godzilla*'s cast are able to figure out a solution to avoid destruction (for the time being) and secure a happy ending that shows that sometimes (rarely) society can work.

The struggle against disaster is most often presented as a physical struggle, one that concerns protecting the body from a physical other, be it the cold or a giant monster, and thus it mostly flirts with films of survival and escape. However, there are a number of disaster films that share their DNA with transformation films. These are films that focus not on the transformative effects of sickness on the body but with reacting to the contagion or pathogen on a larger scale, either by trying to handle it through medical teams and governmental interference or by struggling to get through a world of sickness without getting infected. For those films that focus on the effects of the sickness on the individual's body we'll have to turn to transformation.

Transformation

Times are good for Bob again and the hunt has been plentiful. But not all dangers come from outside. A member of the hunt scratches himself on some thorns, another eats one of the new mushrooms as a quick snack. Everything goes well but by supper time one of the two is feeling sick. He rests early. By the morning he is covered in sores, blisters, rash ... he is not the man he had been the day before. He has become something else. And whether it was through witchcraft or natural means is up for grabs in the community. All that is understood, all that Bob understands now is that the body itself can twist and morph into an abject horror.

Transformation keeps us in the realm of the physical but positions our own bodies as the site of abjection, an inescapable beast, with us no matter where we hide. That alone is a terrifying thought, one that we don't often like to explore in our waking hours but a fear that surfaces every time a loved one gets cancer, every time a cold goes around work. But with the advent of modern medicine, we are living longer than ever and, perhaps unremarkable sounding, we know what is killing us when we finally do bite it. We have not conquered death but we understand it and its origins. It is through films of transformation that we are able to return to the other worldly and terrifying roots of transformation.

We have myths of werewolves, the Norse berserkers thought to be part man, part animal—there are mind bending ways we have thought reality can be played with. And there are sicknesses like the black plague that horribly disfigured those unfortunate souls who were infected. In horror we see these different forms of transformation in films about were-animals such as *Ginger Snaps* (2000) and *An American Werewolf in London* (1981); films that distort the edges of the human body by means of psychedelia like *Videodrome* (1983) and *From Beyond*; and films of infectious disease like *Contracted* (2013), *Antiviral* (2012), *Cabin Fever* (2002) and many of the more intimate zombie films. Often questions of just what exactly it means to be human are asked in transformation. Other times they are used metaphorically to represent real life transformations such as female coming of age in *Ginger Snaps*.

Transformation is all about the between (liminal) state: being one thing turning into something else. It is in that middle ground that they place their focus and explore ideas of the metaphorical and the physical through our inescapable bodies. These films show us what happens when we eat that mushroom or we're strung by the wrong bug. These films take the horror of illness away from our 21st century of Googling diagnoses and violently injects us back into the realm of the mythical and the strange that we developed beyond.

Madness

Bob has struggled through hell on earth by this point in his life; perhaps if I were a kinder creator he might have had a kinder lot. But that wasn't what Bob was created for. His was to be a rough existence. Among the many things that have taken loved ones away from Bob, there has always been one that stood out, one that was different from the rest. Friends might die of cuts and cold but there was a different kind of pain in the world. One that came from within, driving the poor soul further away from the tribe despite their flesh remaining present. It is the enemy not of the flesh but of the mind, that one that lurks at the corners of Bob's mind even now.

The struggle of madness is fought within the mind of the individual. There might be a physical threat through combination with another of the struggles, however the primary arena is for the sanity of the protagonist. This does not mean that sanity is not being tested by an outside source, such as could be argued with *The Haunting* (1963). However, the danger to the protagonist is a threat against their stability of mind—a threat which also sees the protagonists putting their physical selves into harm's way like *The Haunting* and *The Innkeepers* (2011). Both of the examples mentioned have involved the supernatural.

The supernatural is not inherent within films of madness but the two share a close relationship which makes sense upon reflection. Much like tales of transformation take us back to the realm of the unknown in regards to physical transformation, films of madness are the flip side of that coin. The only difference here is that our cultural relationship with mental illness has been so severely fucked up as to present mental illness as both the ultimate unknowable evil or the most complete bullshit ever made up. We don't need to travel nearly as far back in history to find why tales of madness connect with us. We are all of us mad in a world that refuses to understand itself.

Films of madness often blur the lines between reality and delusion. It's no surprise at the end of a film of madness when we learn our primary narrator was unreliable, that the threat we thought was outside was situated within, and that the cycle of insanity is to repeat throughout the decades. Films like *Cat People* and *Jacob's Ladder* (1990) ask you to join them in a mystery, into the mind of madness, into a world gone completely insane where demons walk and women are panthers in disguise. This blurring of reality and fiction, truth and madness, serves to position films of madness within a liminal space between the two; these films' structure and design often take cues from the very madness it suggests: shadows hide truths, the films themselves becoming a reflection of the madness they focus in on, in this way, inviting the viewer to share in the confusion and insanity surrounding the tale.

Not every film of madness is so comprehensively designed, however. Tales of madness can come in disturbingly medical tones, a sterile approach through which to examine madness under the microscope. A good example of this is the 'possession' film *Requiem* (2006). A film of this nature would most often be played with the mystery of, "Is she truly possessed or is this all in her head?" Instead, *Requiem* makes no attempt to convince you of the validity of the possession, instead it focuses on the melancholy one feels watching a loved one suffer. This is madness stripped of its mystical and supernatural powers, it is purely human suffering with no recourse—we're merely along for the trip.

Regardless of which approach to madness the Scream Writer takes, these stories open themselves up to a wide array of thematic readings. Much like a monster is rarely just a monster, insanity is rarely just insanity. Madness may serve as a simple catch-all way to explain a serial killer's actions but frequently madness is used to explore the root causes of madness itself, the treatment of mental illness within society, the abuses of the past arising in the present, and many more. It is for this reason I ask that you give madness some serious thought before employing it in your tales. It holds a power that deserves respect.

Menace

We come at last to menace, the most interesting of the struggles (if, perhaps, the most unpleasant as well). Films of menace are not wholly unique to the horror genre but it is within horror that they find the most representation.

At this point, the pressures on Bob's mind have won and the caveman we once knew is no longer there. Bob is now a brutal serial killer, picking off the weak and the lonesome. Nobody suspects Bob, the darkness holds horrors after all. But, from our privileged position as observers, we know exactly what Bob does; exactly how much suffering he causes. No longer are we scared of what will happen to Bob but of what Bob will do, the hurt he will cause. He is now a menace.

Films of menace are all about giving the audience that privileged view of a monster that can't be stopped. The police don't seem to be able to get them. Even against all the odds, they seem to stack up an unlimited body count. Of course, let's not see the menace as purely a physical

208

figure. The menace is often destructive, either aggressively or reactionarily; however, while often within the realm of the physical, the menace can also be targeting the mental health of its victims.

Films of menace are the only of the struggles to feature an archetypal character, the menace themselves. Madness, transformation, survival, the previous six struggles are adaptable to any characters the Scream Writer wants to create. In contrast, films of menace take the monster from Chapter 2 and set them in the role of protagonist. Through menace the monster transforms, from an entity that fuels a change in the protagonist's life, into an entity that actively works to cause changes in the world itself (a protagonist): the serial killer is no longer a freak encounter but one that actively seeks out victims; the monster is no longer brought into our lives through our actions, visiting the ancient ruins or reading the sacred text, but one that finds us through its own means. In this way, films of menace are often the most disturbing of the struggles.

The most common presentation of menace is in the serial killer subgenre, particularly exemplified by *Henry*, *Maniac* (1980), and *Schramm* (1993). These films give us horrific serial killers as protagonists. The journeys of these three killers come to rest at different conclusions (killer survives/dies) and vary wildly on their interests in exploring the psychology of the different menaces, but the crux of the films are the same. Simply put these films say, "Here is a psychopath. Let's watch." Variations on the format and style brought us the found footage takes of

C'est arrivé près de chez vous (*Man Bites Dog*, 1992) and *The Last Horror Movie* (2003), and the theme has covered more than serial killers as exemplified by the ripped-from-the-headlines fears of *Zero Day* (2003).

However, not every menace film focuses on monsters. The revenge film, whether pure revenge or rape-revenge, is also a form of menace. In these films—*Revenge* (2017), *Ms. 45* (1981), *I Spit on Your Grave* (1978), *Mandy* (2018)—we follow a character that is wronged: they've been raped, left for dead, a witness to their loved one's deaths. These films typically turn from survival to menace, the time spent on survival thus justifying the ruthless violence of menace. In this way the characters in these films of menace are not the monsters, though if it weren't for the survival elements of the first act they most certainly would be. After the survival introduction, the actions of the menacing characters are no less brutal than those monsters that share their struggle.

Combining Struggles

As we've been exploring the seven struggles of horror, we have seen how they are combined to create different responses within the viewer. Survival before menace allows us to connect with the menace; transformation, survival, and escape are often combined together within the zombie film. In laying out these struggles it's important to make note of how to make use of them to the best of your ability.

No screenwriter sits down and begins with the question, "Is this a film about survival or a film about transformation?" The ideas for stories come from all over: an interesting monster, a chance encounter on the street, the way a leaf looks as it floats on the wind. I believe that as Scream Writers we should follow the story and see how far it will take us. But often we will run into roadblocks; for whatever reason we can't seem to get the cognitive effect we want out of the story or even just a scene. It is when we get stuck that we need to remember just how primal our emotions really are.

What struggle are you tapping into? What is it being used to make the audience feel? Is it the best struggle for that or could it be paired with another to deepen the intended effect? Our characters, our politics, our style, voice, tone, all are layers that we add on top of these struggles: they are the building blocks that we rest upon the foundation of struggle.

Through this process the building of our stories is a form of transforming the struggle through a personal lens that sees the combination of the Scream Writer with the struggle. The very act of storytelling is an act of combination, so do not be afraid to mix and play with struggles to create new and interesting formats. Not everything can be paired together, attempts to provoke two distinct cognitive effects may only result in provoking a third, unexpected, result. But a solid understanding of the anxieties that we are tapping into allows us to be precise and deliberate with the emotional bids in our screamplays.

<u>Story Structure</u>

When I was first learning to write, I hated the very idea of structure. The thought of boiling down the elusive nature of creativity into some sort of framework or hierarchy was blasphemy to my anarchist mind. However, as I continue to study stories and practice brainstorming in collaborative environments I have come to find that story structure truly is the glue that holds everything together.

However, I have also come to find that I dislike 90% of the writing out there on story structure. Everyone has a preferred structure that they want to hook you on; if you listen to them and your movie ends up getting made and, heaven forbid, winning awards then that is proof that they're particular recipe is the right one. I believe that each story should have a structure that makes sense for that particular tale. In order to prevent myself from becoming another voice claiming to have the right answer, we will first explore the structures that Syd Field and Dan Harmon have identified (both useful but too specific) and then explore two of the personal story structures I have had fun using as a way to showcase a variety of approaches.

<u>Syd Field's Paradigm</u>

Mr. Field has been writing on the topic of screenwriting and story structure since the late 1970s when he released *Screenplay: The Foundations of Screenwriting*. He continued to teach on the subject until his death in 2013 and is one of the most respected thinkers on the subject. I personally own a copy of *The Screenwriter's Workbook* that is littered with Post-It notes. However, I disagree with Mr. Field about the specificity of his writings on story structure. Mr. Field was a script reader during the '70s and his focus on specificity can best be explored in this quote from Steven Price's *A History of the Screenplay*:

> … their excessive specificity. For example, not only does Field insist that screenplays have three acts ('setup', 'confrontation' and 'resolution'), but acts one and two should also have a 'plot point', which 'is an incident, or event, that hooks into the story and spins it around into another direction'. Because Field has confidence in the one-page-per-minute rule, this leads him to the remarkably precise assertion that in a screenplay for a two-hour film the first and third acts should be 30 pages each, with the middle act occupying 60 pages; the plot points, meanwhile, should occur around pages 25-27 and 85-90. For Field, then, not

only acts but also plot points are not matters of
interpretation; they are scientifically measurable
… another cause for concern is that Field,
Chrisopher Vogler, Robert McKee and others were
not themselves noted screenwriters, but instead
began as studio readers … it would be more
accurate to say … that "the screenplay manuals
were guilding hopefuls to write scripts that would
galvanize the frontline reader (206)

The specificity of these manuals make the thought of
screenwriting much more complicated than it should be.
However, if one is primarily interested in being produced
through Hollywood and the studio system in place, Mr.
Field's writings offer a solid path to a well trodden
structure. Mr. Field's particular structure is three acts with
the middle divided into two pieces. So in reality it is a
four act structure with different stakes attached to the two
acts of confrontation.

A screenplay following Mr. Field's structure spends the
first thirty pages setting up the world and introduces the
characters. A plot point at the end of this act pulls us into
the first half of the second act which is then connected to
the second part of act two through a midpoint event that
changes the spin of the second act. This second act is our
act of confrontation in which stakes continue to rise and
actions to solve the complications are taken (often to the
protagonists detriment). Plot point two takes links the
third act in which the final confrontation is driven by the

protagonist and concludes the story. Through this a chain of connection keeps the various acts held firmly together. Let's see how a film like *Leprechaun 2* (1994) would be set forth in Mr. Field's paradigm.

The first act introduces us to the idea that the Leprechaun is after a bride and quickly sets forth a bit of mythology about how that happens. It also introduces us to the Leprechaun, our main character Cody, his and the Leprechaun's love interest Bridget, and some supporting cast. When Bridget is kidnapped by the Leprechaun we have the plot point that carries us into the second act where Cody works to rescue Bridget. Cody's quasi-mentor and alcoholic boss Morty seems to know how to trick the Leprechaun and it seems like everything is going to be okay because of a good ol' fashion Irish drinking contest. This is the midpoint act that sees them lose the Leprechaun and have to go after him again. Having finally caught the little bastard, the second plot point to carry us into the third act is the death of Morty, or Cody's lowest point emotionally. Here Cody has only one chance to save Bridget and it is through a direct confrontation and his storming the castle (or a cave as it was here), slaying the dragon and rescuing the princess finish the third act.

In sitting down to explore how *Leprechaun 2* fits into Mr. Field's paradigm I was met with a more challenging task than I expected. First I wanted to use *Videodrome* as my example but then the question was "What is plot point one?" Is it when he first sees the videodrome transmission? Is it when he begins to date Nicki? Is it the first hallucination? And what is the middle point? Is it finding out that O'Blivion is dead? Being brainwashed? Nicki going missing? It blurs quite a few lines. I had similar problems with *Leprechaun 2* in identifying that middle point. What event truly marks a change? The film doesn't truly have a middle point but rather its second act is an escalation. What is that escalation? Well, *Leprechaun 2* might not be the best example because it can be so hard to take seriously but it is ultimately a rising of the stakes and a tightening of the tension. Characters are dying, things only get worse, like most horror it is a nightmare in its own abstract way (but not to the degree of a film like *Suspiria*).

In the specificity that Mr. Field lays out you can see a great deal many dramas and thrillers but the horror film is a little more elusive, it plays by its own rules and is often quite a bit shorter than the numbers that Mr. Field lays out. While his structure presents a solid grounding for the beginning screenwriter, it is too rigid to keep up with the changing nature of filmmaking and the rise of the independent market's flexibility around film length.

Dan Harmon's Story Circle

Mr. Harmon takes a lot of influence from the works of comparative mythologist Joseph Campbell, particularly his monomyth or "hero's journey," in his grounding as a screenwriter. As one of the leading minds behind Channel

101, a monthly short film festival he started along with Rob Schrab, Mr. Harmon sets out his version of story structure which is in the form of a circle. In this way, Mr. Harmon believes that the path of most stories (though he will be the first to admit there are exceptions to every rule of storytelling) follow a circular motion so that the character finishes where they started from but having grown through the experience. Where Mr. Field saw four acts with three key plot points, Mr. Harmon identifies eight key points in his structure:

1. You (a character is in a zone of comfort)
2. Need (but they want something)
3. Go (they enter an unfamiliar situation)
4. Search (adapt to it)
5. Find (find what they wanted)
6. Take (pay its price)
7. Return (and go back to where they started)
8. Change (now capable of change)

(Channel101.Fandom.com)

You first introduce us to the character, then you show us that something isn't right in their world and that they have a desire. In order to solve this need they have to go out of their comfort zone where they find out that in order to succeed they are going to have to adapt to the new level of homeostasis this area requires. Then comes part five which Mr. Harmon likens to Mr. Field's midpoint. Mr. Harmon sees this as the opposite of point one, the comfort zone. Here the point is that there is a definable moment related to a change within the character. It represents the point in the story in which your character is able to fit himself into the shape of what they need to be.

In part six, Mr. Harmon identifies that having now reached the point of having what they needed, the character now must begin a second road of trials, that of the road back home. Therefore six is often where the protagonist gets their ass kicked regardless of the gains from five. In a romantic-comedy this is where the lovers typically break up. In return we often see physical movement as a key, as Mr. Harmon points out by identifying this as a great point for a car chase, the misunderstood lover rushing to beat the plane that'll take away their one true love. This is the opposite of crossing the threshold and it brings the protagonist to the point where they can kill the bad guy or save their relationship. Let's see how my personal favorite, *The Evil Dead*, looks in Mr. Harmon's Story Circle.

Our protagonist is Ash Williams, who begins the film in a place of comfort as he travels to a cabin in the woods for a weekend with his friends and his girlfriend. Exploring the basement, Ash and Scotty find a tape recorder and the necronomicon ex mortis, loosely translated 'The Book of the Dead.' The finding of the book represents the second part of the circle but as is often the case in horror it is almost the film, or rather the horror elements within it, that are working on the characters. Ash's need is not to listen to the tape, but the need of the tape is to be listened to and thus we follow its need instead. This leads to the possession of Ash's sister and throws out hurdling over the threshold.

Ash is too afraid to attack Cheryl when she is assaulting Scotty and so Ash's adventure is search is one for courage and strength which sees him find his nerve, through which he can use the shotgun as a weapon, and he is able to dispatch his possessed girlfriend. But the discovery of his ability to find back forces him back into the cellar to get more shotgun cells, thus leading him back to where this all began and bringing him to a confrontation with his sister in which he uses the shotgun. However, Ash does not make a return trip here. Rather, it is the now possessed Scotty that returns from death in order to bring Ash into the final confrontation in which he is able to defeat monsters and returns to the front of the cabin and the car that he began the movie in.

Where Mr. Harmon's story circle is able to fit quite fluidly to many films, horror again proves to complicate it to a degree. This is because horror is often about corrupting this journey—more often than not horror is more interested in taking away a character's power and ruining their place of comfort so as to make it unreturnable. I like Mr. Harmon's Story Circle for its flexibility with how individual events are paced and explored but when it comes to horror it leaves room for expansion.

My Experimentation

I strongly believe that story structure is of importance in developing our stories but I believe that structure can be experimented with in ways that produce a deliberate and calculated cognitive effect from the viewer. In my experimentations with structure not everything has worked and some ideas have had to be scrapped entirely. But what comes out of this practice is a better understanding of the ways in which stories can be told and how truly amazing and flexible the format can be. In order to get to this place I recommend first beginning with explorations in more typical structures as exemplified within the writings of Syd Field, Dan Harmon, Robert McKee, Blake Synder, et. al.

Similarities pop up throughout these writings but so too does a great deal of variance. I want to implore you to think with variance when it comes to your storytelling, to find unique ways of exploring story and character. Here are two examples of divergent story structures that I have played with and found great satisfaction in using.

Together, me and my friend and fellow writer Kelly Warner have been developing a film that we describe as Carpenter's *Prince of Darkness* meets Scorsese's *Silence* (2016). It is the story of a priest offering aid to a small village in the jungle where the site of a pre-man religion is unearthed. Contact with the priest and the village is cut off and an expedition is sent into the jungle to ascertain the situation.

To accomplish our aims we designed the plot in the manner of a Russian nesting doll. In the outermost layer of our structure are three acts. Then there is a three act structure nested within the grand second and third act. Again we see this on a smaller scale as our third grand third act holds within it three acts. This can be visualized like so:

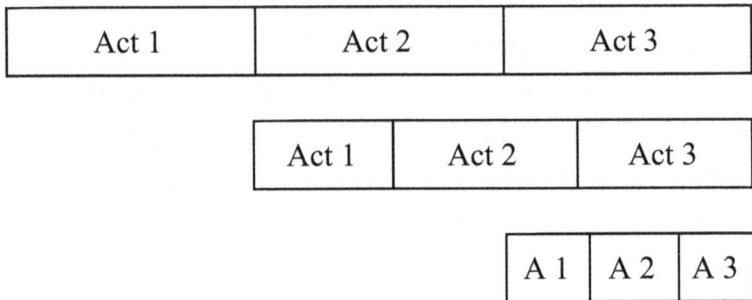

Act 1	Act 2	Act 3

	Act 1	Act 2	Act 3

		A 1	A 2	A 3

This was a very fun way of layering the story. What we knew is that the character we identify with in the first act disappears for the second and returns in the third. Act two introduces us to the characters that will go searching for him, so in a way it uses a sped up version of the act one set up. The story then continues with those characters until the end and they experience their experience is divided into three acts easily.

Then as a way to continually keep our third act ramping, it first functions as the conclusion to what act one sets up with the priest that goes missing as well as the culmination to the three acts started in act two but it also follows a breakneck three act pace. In this way Kelly and I have taken aspects of the anthology film but used them to tell a singular story as a series of key situations that all feed into each other but also stand as stories of their own right.

The other structure that I have had a lot of fun using is triangular in nature. In this script I wanted to explore alternative ways of telling a revenge story and borrowed heavily from the structure of Simon Rumley's 2010 masterpiece *Red, White & Blue*. Here I am telling the story of an elderly gentleman that is swarmed by a group of adolescents while walking home through the park at night (unfortunately inspired by news from my city). My first act focuses on the elderly man's story of being beaten and how violence is the option he settles on to face his fear of youth. The second act then abandons the old man to follow one of the youths that assaulted him. The old man makes a violent return in act three which sees him violently attack the youths.

This is triangular in nature because instead of following the events set up in the first act, the story jumps back and offers a second first act before moving into the concluding third. Act one and two make up the two points at the base of the triangle, both are connected through a flat line that represents their nature as set up—the foundation of the story. But both point towards the third act, the top of the triangle, with their long reaching arms suggesting violence. What this has done is take a two act story, man is hurt so man causes violence, and delay the payoff through pointing the lens away from our victim (as is typical with the revenge genre) to instead see the perpetrator's point of view.

In this way I have avoided the second act which typically sees the protagonist preparing for their violent spree and gaining the confidence needed, and instead have put the focus on seeing both sides of the story so as to offer compassion to both. In this way the story is of a much slower pace, more in tune with the films of Bergman than with the horror of a Carpenter or Craven, and in doing so have increased the emotional potency of the violence within the film.

So please, practice exploring how films and screenplays line up to different structures, they offer a skeleton upon which to build your stories. Just don't be tricked into thinking the skeleton always has to be human.

Horror and Plot

There is an endless amount of writing on the subject of plot and it's my desire to avoid rehashing things that have been said a thousand times. Instead I want to close up on some thoughts about plot specific to horror.

<u>The Human Element</u>

When it comes to horror we often see this idea floating around on popular media websites: horror is not about characters, themes, or depth; horror is about scaring you and that is it. This is a reductionist approach to the horror genre that does it a great disservice in its ability to portray the deepest of human emotions. Films like *Hereditary*, horror films with a focus on the family and the interpersonal relationships between them, are often called out as "not being horror." More surprising is that a film like *The Nun* would get the same sort of lash back, at least in Twitter discussions that Bloody Disgusting's John Squires has spoken about. Even the latest version of Stephen King's *It* (2017) was called out as not being horror and that's a movie about a demonic killer clown that is actually a shapeshifting entity from another dimension.

I guess what I'm trying to say is that this view of horror is bullshit.

Horror has always been able to explore the deeply psychological problems of its characters. Just look at *The Cabinet of Dr. Caligari* and how the story reveals itself to be a reflection of a psychotic character's inner mind. Look at how *The Exorcist* explores faith, family bonds, the frailty of science. With all of its lofty themes it has been the recipient of nearly as much film scholarship as the works of Tarkovsky or Bergman; but at the core of the film are the struggles of a priest to refind his religion and the story of a family being torn apart by illness. It is haunting and terrifying in its depiction of medical testing, let alone all the demonic elements that are brought into the film.

Because of the overwhelming stress and weirdness of the situations that make up horror, these stories prove time and time again to be the perfect way to explore the elements that make up our lives: physical, psychological, social, cultural, and, of course, the primal. *It Follows* is the story of the rocky sexual awakening of a teenage girl. *Possession* examines the disintegration of a marriage through some of the most horrific images of horror ever captured on film (primarily thanks to the amazing performances of Sam Neill and especially Isabelle Adjani). Often what horror is doing is taking these concepts and investing them into another form. In this way the emotional experience of the characters—for example the stresses of sexual awakening in *It Follows*—are given a literal form that allows the character's internal struggles to be perceived in a physical form.

Not every horror film has to give a physical form in order to give meaning to the characters, however. The best horror movies are often regular stories of people going through typical dramatic situations—break ups, pregnancy, dealing with trauma, betrayal, etc.—and a horror element is dropped into that story. In this way the stakes of the story are raised but the emotional connection to the characters is gained through our identification with their struggles and hardships. When the stakes are raised, the dramatic elements of the story typically begin to move at a breakneck pace (this is not always the case, but even a fair share of slow burn horror has an elevated third act pace).

In all stories, the human element is the most important for giving depth and meaning and, most importantly, connection to your audience. Just because your story is more than a series of murder vignettes does not mean it is not horror.

Horror is human.

Hidden Meanings

Horror shares with sci-fi an incredible elasticity in regards to holding meaning. Throughout the history of film we see, time and time again, filmmakers using the horror genre as a way to critique the dominant political party and cultural values. Because horror is one of the genres of the fantastique, the elements that it brings in (ghosts, goblins, monsters, oh my) are sponges for meaning. We talked about this when we spoke about monsters as metaphors. However here I want to look a little bit more broadly.

One of the things that filmmakers have been doing since forever now is shooting movies in foreign countries as a way to speak about their own. Jess Franco famously set his films outside of Spain so he could reflect his political views of the ruling party by having foreign government agents represent his own. This approach was followed by Jorge Grau who's police inspector in *The Living Dead at the Manchester Morgue* (1974) speaks more about Spanish police than it does the British.

Likewise, some meanings are so blatant that to write about them under the label of hidden might seem out of place but they hide in plain sight. The perfect example of this is the predatory sexual abuse of *Starry Eyes*. In the film our lead character, Sarah, is a wannabe actress. She hangs out with her friends, works a dead end job waiting tables, but she strives to land that one role that will change everything. In order to get the role Sarah has to abuse herself, perform sexual favours for the producer, and, ultimately, kill her friends and be reborn. In order to be reborn she must first wither and rot.

In this, the film focuses on the horrors of Hollywood, a couple years before the #MeToo movement was to catch momentum and make these issues a talking point in popular culture. It also suggests that the cost of fame is the death of who you once were and a violent rupturing of the social circle you can no longer be a part of. *Starry Eyes* doesn't particular hide its meaning but it is diffused through lens of murder and body horror. In this way the concepts and the emotional pain associated with the road to fame is given a physical manifestation, one that speaks to the filmmakers own thoughts on the idea through its abject imagery.

Momentum

When it comes to pacing there tends to be two approaches that dominate the horror genre. The first is the steady ramp, which sees the momentum of the film increases exponentially. The second is the slow burn, which may see an exponential increase in the momentum of the film but not always (and if so it is a much more gradual curve). As we've seen through an exploration of story structure, this is not always the case. However, it is often enough that these two approaches deserve some consideration.

The steady ramp film typically identifies itself with an opening scene of horror to catch the audience's attention right off the bat. This scene screams, "Hey, this is what kind of movie you're in for," and carries the film through the first act set up. The steady ramp then continues to escalate throughout the second act, things constantly get worse and worse and worse. In these films a victory is never long lasting because to dwell in victory is to allow the pace to slow. The ramp lends itself best to films of survival, menace, and disaster because these struggles require the most reactionary responses from the protagonists.

The third act in these films tend to be explosive and consist of a showdown between the protagonists and the antagonists that is rooted in the realm of the physical: think the chases at the end of slasher films; Otto's death in *Henry*; the fight with Spike in *Gremlins* or the final confrontation in man versus animal films. These films build and build until confrontation is the only possible end. Slasher films are the perfect example of the steady ramp film: they were often given writing demands that there be a kill every ten minutes, and as the cast of characters dimensions the film pushes towards a final confrontation and often (though not always) increases the rate of killings going into the third act.

In contrast, the slow burn films tend to focus less on events and more on the internal world of the characters. In this way, these films are particularly suited to transformation and madness (with menace and escape following behind). The slow burn is about gradually laying the pieces of the story down, exploring how the characters react to them. This slower pace means that the third act is often not nearly as explosive as the third acts of steady ramp films; however, this is not always the truth and sometimes the purpose of the slow burn was to earn an explosive finish. Often if your third act goes completely off the wheels—thinking of you *Hereditary*—then you want to make sure that you have brought the audience into the story world and have fostered connection to the characters so that by the time you jeer off the rails the audience is already buckled in for the ride.

While steady ramp films are the easiest to see how they slot into a particular story structure, the slow burn requires a little more thought. The physicality that propels the steady ramp film means that often their plot points are focused around an identifiable action: the hunt for the killer; the confrontation with the police; the kidnapping, etc. The plot points of slow burn films are often centered on the discovery of information (either through research or dialogue) or in the emotional aspects of an event, in this way building out the world of the story.

This is not always the case.

Hereditary is a slow burn film in which a death is the major plot point (though it spins the film into a focus on how the characters handle their grief). Though steady ramp and slow burn films tend to focus on physicality and information in their plot points, the best of these films find ways of combining both so that the story continues to have a sense of movement. This is especially important in the slow burn film, a sense of movement is necessary in conjunction with the slower pace or the story will feel sluggish.

Triggering Events

Both Syd Field and Dan Harmon identify the idea that characters begin in a start of comfort which is then left.

Mr. Harmon identifies the leaving of the comfort zone as the journey to fulfill a need. Mr. Field sees this as the first plot point of the movie, the thing that carries the story into the second act and thus the primary action. In horror Mr. Field's first plot point functions far easily as our triggering event.

Within horror our protagonists don't just leave their comfort zone, they have it violently torn away from them. Often the very zone that was to give them comfort is perverted so as to cause them misery. In this the horror works against our characters and demands reaction from them. Frodo may have been able to say, "No, I won't transport the ring," in *Lord of the Rings*, but Laurie has no power of Michael's action. No character goes out seeking horror (except in films of menace).

Horror must rupture its way into their world: it is the werewolves in *Dog Soldiers*; the deadites of *The Evil Dead*; the possession in *The Exorcist*; the shark in *Jaws*; and perhaps it is no more literal than the chestburster in *Alien* (though at a different plot point). The goals and desires of our characters may still matter (should still matter) but their world is completely altered by the horror elements. In this way the nerdy kid is able to prove that his knowledge of monsters was a strength; the lovers are pushed closer together through their need for teamwork.

The triggering event is often a complete surprise. Regan's possession is a complete surprise in terms of the story—sure, the movie is called *The Exorcist* so we know a possession is gonna happen but why her? Why now?

The werewolves of *Dog Soldiers* are a complete surprise, narratively. The randomness of Saskia's disappearance in *Spoorloos* (*The Vanishing*, 1988); Frank's resurrection in *Hellraiser* (1987); *Cujo* (1983) catching rabies; these events are all surprises that change the direction of the story and present horror's rupture into the world. While the promotional materials may explicitly highlight what the surprise is, the narrative presents it as a complete shift. While the vast majority of films have the triggering event as a surprise, this is not always true. *Candyman* sets up the mythology of the character (say his name in the mirror, he comes) and so it is not a surprise when Candyman appears when called. Not for the audience, or narratively, but it is still a surprise for the character because only a non-believer could have the gall to call forth their own murderer.

While the horror-comedy *The Cabin in the Woods* would at first seem to complicate this idea of surprise, a further examination reveals the importance of surprise in the triggering event. In the film a cast of 20-somethings take a vacation to a cabin in the woods, not realizing that the cabin, the trip, and everything that follows has all been set up by a corporation that is monitoring the characters and turning their lives into a horror movie. The triggering act comes with the awakening of the zombie family that will attack them. Our characters find their way into the basement of the cabin where this is just a ton of weird and unique objects on display.

Our company men watch from their headquarters, taking bets on which object they will pick. What the company men know is that each object will awaken a different monster. Because we are connected to the company men, we are narratively prepared for what will happen and thus the surprise of the monster is gone. However, much like *Candyman*, the characters in the cabin are unaware of what they are getting into and so the event is a surprise to them. However, surprise is further layered into the film by the company men's betting pool on which monster will be selected. They know that a monster will be picked but they know not which and therefore neither do we the audience. In this way *The Cabin in the Woods* highlights the importance of surprise in the triggering event while giving the appearance of having stripped it away.

Exercises

1. Look at five of your favorite horror movies and list the struggles that they employ. Do they focus on one or do they mix and match to create a new experience?

2. What is the structure of your Scream Play? If you haven't thought about it yet, explore how it fits into Mr. Field or Mr. Harmon's structures. Can you identify where your first act ends and the second begins? How about the point that moves it into the third?

3. List out your plot beats, if you don't know what constitutes a plot beat list out the major moments in your story. Is the action being driven by your characters? Horror first acts upon our characters, injecting itself into their world, but it is through their reactions and choices that the audience is brought into caring about them and identifying with them. If your character is constantly being acted upon, then it's time to make them more assertive.

<u>Conclusion</u>

It has been a journey but we're finally at the end. I hope that in exploring the various elements that we use within horror you have made new discoveries and given thought to areas that you had been neglecting. In laying the parts out as I have, I have tried my best to avoid "absolute" rules—where that has been implied accidentally, it's my hope that you take to heart that rules are meant to be broken. Each story is unique and the way you tell it is entirely up to you and it.

While I still have you here, I want to quickly revisit something I mentioned in the introduction. Writing is supposed to be fun. We're all of us drawn to screenwriting because of the films we watched and the stories they told. Something was moved within you and you realized you wanted to (maybe even had to) tell your own story through film. Some of us have been writing so long we forgot just how powerful it was, how exciting its pull was. And some of us have turned our writing into a career and it's easy to lose sight of the joy when it becomes a source of income.

But writing is supposed to be fun. That's why it's terribly upsetting just how many writers suffer from depression or think less of themselves because of their relationship to their creativity. Regardless if it is horror, melodrama, action or sci-fi, your stories matter. The tales you tell are important. Only you have the ability to tell a story the way you do. That is a beautiful, wonderful thing. I hope you remember that next time writing has got you down.

Bibliography

Blatty, William Peter. *Classic Screenplays: The Exorcist & Legion*. London, England, Faber & Faber, 1998.

Cameron, James. "Terminator (1982)." The Daily Script, https://www.dailyscript.com.

Caroll, Noel. *The Philosophy of Horror, or Paradoxes of the Heart*. Routledge, 1990.

Clover, Carol J. "Her Body, Himself: Gender in the Slasher Film". *Representations*, No. 20, Special Issue: Misogyny, Misandry, and Misanthropy (Autumn, 1987), pp. 187-228.

Coleridge, Samuel Taylor. *Biographia Literaria*. (1817) Edited by Nigel Leask. London, J. M. Dent, 1997.

Ebert, Roger. "Night of the Living Dead." RogerEbert.com, www.rogerebert.com/reviews/the-night-of-the-living-dead-1968.

Ebert, Roger. "The Exorcist." RogerEbert.com, www.rogerebert.com/reviews/the-exorcist-1973.

Grant, Barry Keith. "Screams on Screens: Paradigms of Horror." *Special Issue—Thinking After Dark: Welcome to the World of Horror Video Games,* vol. 4, no. 6, 2010, journals.sfu.ca/loading/index.php/loading/article/view/85.

Harmon, Dan. "Story Structure 101: Super Basic Shit." Channel101,

www.channel101.fandom.com/wiki/Story_Structure_101:
_Super_Basic_Shit.

Hill, Walter, and David Giler. "Alien (1978)." The Daily Script, https://www.dailyscript.com.

Jackson, Kimberly. *Gender and the Nuclear Family in Twenty-First-Century Horror*. Palgrave Macmillan, 2015.

Vander Kaay, Chris, and Kathleen Fernandez-. *Horror Films by Subgenre: A Viewer's Guide*. McFarland, 2016.

Kahneman, Daniel. *Thinking, Fast and Slow*. Farrar, Straus and Giroux, 2013.

Kristeva, Julia. *Powers of Horror: An Essay on Abjection*. Columbia University Press, 1982.

Lancaster, Bill. "The Thing (1982)." The Daily Script, https://www.dailyscript.com.

Marriott, James, and Kim Newman. *Horror!: 333 Films to Scare You to Death*. Carlton Books, 2010.

Ochoa, George. *Deformed and Destructive Beings: The Purpose of Horror Films*. McFarland, 2011.

Oxford English Dictionary. Oxford University Press, 2012.

Pinker, Steven. *The Better Angels of Our Nature: Why Violence Has Declined*. Penguin Books, 2012.

Price, Steven. *A History of the Screenplay*. Palgrave Macmillan, 2013.

Truffaut, François. *Hitchcock*. Simon & Schuster, 1985.

Winter, Douglas. *Prime Evil*. Dutton Adult, 1981.

Filmography

10 Cloverfield Lane (2016) – Director: Dan Trachtenberg. Screenplay: Josh Campbell, Matt Stuecken and Damien Chazell.

10 Rillington Place (1971) – Director: Richard Fleischer. Screenplay: Clive Exton.

1408 (2007) – Director: Mikael Håfström. Screenplay: Matt Greenberg, Scott Alexander and Larry Karaszewski.

28 Days Later (2002) – Director: Danny Boyle. Screenplay: Alex Garland.

À L'intérieur (*Inside*, 2007) – Director: Julien Maury and Alexandre Bustillo. Screenplay: Alexandre Bustillo.

A Nightmare on Elm Street (1984) – Director: Wes Craven. Screenplay: Wes Craven

Aaahh!!! Real Monsters (1994-1997, TV) – Created by: Gábor Csupó and Peter Gaffney.

Alien (1979) – Director: Ridley Scott. Screenplay: Dan O'Bannon.

An American Werewolf in London (1981) – Director: John Landis. Screenplay: John Landis.

An Inconvenient Truth (2006) – Director: Davis Guggenheim. Written by: Al Gore.

Annabelle (2014) – Director: John R. Leonetti. Screenplay: Gary Dauberman.

Antichrist (2009) – Director: Lars von Trier. Screenplay: Lars von Trier.

Antiviral (2012) – Director: Brandon Cronenberg. Screenplay: Brandon Cronenberg.

Apostle (2018) – Director: Gareth Evans. Screenplay: Gareth Evans.

Arachnid (2001) – Director: Jack Sholder. Screenplay: Mark Sevi.

Arachnophobia (1990) – Director: Frank Marshall. Screenplay: Don Jakoby and Wesley Strick.

Army of Darkness (1993) – Director: Sam Raimi. Screenplay: Sam Raimi and Ivan Raimi.

As Above, So Below (2014) – Director: John Erick Dowdle. Screenplay: John Erick Dowdle.

Assault on Precinct 13 (1976) – Director: John Carpenter. Screenplay: John Carpenter.

Aterrados (*Terrified*, 2017) – Director: Demián Rugna. Screenplay: Demián Rugna.

August Underground's Mordum (2003) – Director: Killjoy, Fred Vogel, Cristie Whiles, Jerami Cruise and Michael Todd Schneider. Screenplay: Killjoy, Fred Vogel, Cristie Whiles, Jerami Cruise and Michael Todd Schneider.

Badlands (1973) – Director: Terrence Malick. Screenplay: Terrence Malick.

Basketcase (1982) – Director: Frank Henenlotter. Screenplay: Frank Henenlotter.

Batman Begins (2005) – Director: Christopher Nolan. Screenplay: Christopher Nolan and David S. Goyer.

Beauty and the Beast (1991) – Director: Gary Trousdale and Kirk Wise. Screenplay: Linda Woolverton.

Biohazard (1985) – Director: Fred Olen Ray. Screenplay: Fred Olen Ray.

Blood and Black Lace (1964) – Director: Mario Bava. Screenplay: Marcello Fondato, Giuseppe Barilla and Maria Bava.

Blood Feast (1963) – Director: Herschell Gordon Lewis. Screenplay: Allison Louise Downe.

Blue Velvet (1986) – Director: David Lynch. Screenplay: David Lynch.

Buffy the Vampire Slayer (1997-2003, TV) – Created by: Joss Whedon.

Cabin Fever (2002) – Director: Eli Roth. Screenplay: Eli Roth and Randy Pearlstein.

Candyman (1992) – Director: Bernard Rose. Screenplay: Bernard Rose.

Carrie (1976) – Director: Brian De Palma. Screenplay: Lawrence D. Cohen.

Cat People (1942) – Director: Jacques Tourneur. Screenplay: DeWitt Bodeen.

Child's Play (1988) – Director: Tom Holland. Screenplay: Don Mancini, John Lafia and Tom Holland.

Clean, Shaven (1993) – Director: Lodge Kerrigan. Screenplay: Lodge Kerrigan.

Cloverfield (2008) – Director: Matt Reeves. Screenplay: Drew Goddard.

Community (2009-2015, TV) – Created: Dan Harmon.

Contagion (2011) – Director: Steven Soderbergh. Screenplay: Scott Z. Burns.

Contracted (2013) – Director: Eric England. Screenplay: Eric England.

Critters (1986) – Director: Stephen Herek. Screenplay: Stephen Herek, Domonic Muir and Don Keith Opper.

Cube (1997) – Director: Vincenzo Natali. Screenplay: André Bijelic, Graeme Manson and Vincenzo Natali.

Cujo (1983) – Director: Lewis Teague. Screenplay: Don Carlos Dunaway and Lauren Currier.

Das Cabinet des Dr. Caligari (*The Cabinet of Dr. Caligari*, 1920) – Director: Robert Wiene. Screenplay: Carl Meyer and Hans Janowitz.

Dawn of the Dead (1978) – Director: George A. Romero. Screenplay: George A. Romero.

Dawn of the Dead (2004) – Director: Zack Snyder. Screenplay: James Gunn.

Death Ship (1980) – Director: Alvin Rakoff. Screenplay: Jack Hill, David P. Lewis and John Robins.

Death Spa (1989) – Director: Michael Fischa. Screenplay: James Bartruff and Mitch Paradise.

Deliverance (1972) – Director: John Boorman. Screenplay: James Dickey.

Dog Soldiers (2002) – Director: Neil Marshall. Screenplay: Neil Marshall.

Dolls (1987) – Director: Stuart Gordon. Screenplay: Ed Naha.

Mais ne Nous Délivrez Pas du Mal (*Don't Deliver Us from Evil*, 1971) – Director: Joël Séria. Screenplay: Joël Séria.

Downrange (2017) – Director: Ryuhei Kitamura. Screenplay: Ryuhei Kitamura and Joey O'Bryan.

Dracula (1931) – Director: Tod Browning. Screenplay: Garrett Fort.

Dracula (1958) – Director: Terence Fisher. Screenplay: Jimmy Sangster.

Dressed to Kill (1980) – Director: Brian De Palma. Screenplay: Brian De Palma.

Duel (1971) – Director: Steven Spielberg. Screenplay: Richard Matheson.

Eden Lake (2008) – Director: James Watkins. Screenplay: James Watkins.

Eight Legged Freaks (2002) – Director: Ellory Elkayem. Screenplay: Ellory Elkayem and Randy Kornfield.

Event Horizon (1997) – Director: Paul W. S. Anderson. Screenplay: Philip Eisner.

Evil Dead (2013) – Director: Fede Álvarez. Screenplay: Fede Álvarez and Rodo Sayagues.

Final Destination (2000–2011, film series)

Frailty (2001) – Director: Bill Paxton. Screenplay: Brent Hanley.

Frankenstein (1931) – Director: James Whale. Screenplay: Francis Edward Faragoh and Garrett Fort.

Freaks (1932) – Director: Tod Browning. Screenplay: Willis Goldbeck and Leon Gordon.

Freddy's Dead: The Final Nightmare (1991) – Director: Rachel Talalay. Screenplay: Michael De Luca.

Friday the 13th (1980) – Director: Sean S. Cunningham. Screenplay: Victor Miller.

Friday the 13th (2009) – Director: Marcus Nispel. Screenplay: Damian Shannon and Mark Swift.

Friday the 13th: The Final Chapter (1984) – Director: Joseph Zito. Screenplay: Barney Cohen.

From Beyond (1986) – Director: Stuart Gordon. Screenplay: Dennis Paoli.

Funny Games (1997, 2007) – Director: Michael Haneke. Screenplay: Michael Haneke.

Ghost (1990) – Director: Jerry Zucker. Screenplay: Bruce Joel Rubin.

Ghostwatch (1992) – Director: Lesley Manning. Screenplay: Stephen Volk.

Ginger Snaps (2000) – Director: John Fawcett. Screenplay: Karen Walton and John Fawcett.

Gojira (*Godzilla*, 1954) – Director: Ishirō Honda. Screenplay: Takeo Murata and Ishirō Honda.

Grave (*Raw*, 2016) – Director: Julia Ducounau. Screenplay: Julia Ducournau.

Green Room (2015) – Director: Jeremy Saulnier. Screenplay: Jeremy Saulnier.

Gremlins (1984) – Director: Joe Dante. Screenplay: Chris Columbus.

Halloween (1978) – Director: John Carpenter. Screenplay: John Carpenter and Debra Hill.

Halloween (2007) – Director: Rob Zombie. Screenplay: Rob Zombie.

Halloween: Resurrection (2002) – Director: Rick Rosenthal. Screenplay: Larry Brand and Sean Hood.

Heavenly Creatures (1994) – Director: Peter Jackson. Screenplay: Peter Jackson and Fran Walsh.

Hellbound: Hellraiser II (1988) – Director: Tony Randel. Screenplay: Peter Atkins.

Hellraiser (1987) – Director: Clive Barker. Screenplay: Clive Barker.

Henry: Portrait of a Serial Killer (1986) – Director: John McNaughton. Screenplay: Richard Fire and John McNaughton.

Hereditary (2018) – Director: Ari Aster. Screenplay: Ari Aster.

Hounds of Love (2016) – Director: Ben Young. Screenplay: Ben Young.

House of 1000 Corpses (2003) – Director: Rob Zombie. Screenplay: Rob Zombie.

House of Usher (1960) – Director: Robert Corman. Screenplay: Richard Matheson.

House on Haunted Hill (1959) – Director: William Castle. Screenplay: Robb White.

House on Haunted Hill (1999) – Director: William Malone. Screenplay: Dick Beebe.

I Am Legend (2007) – Director: Francis Lawrence. Screenplay: Mark Protosevich and Akiva Goldsman.

I Spit on Your Grave (1978) – Director: Meir Zarchi. Screenplay: Meir Zarchi.

I Walked With a Zombie (1943) – Director: Jacques Tourneur. Screenplay: Curt Siodmak and Ardel Wray.

I Was a Teenage Frankenstein (1957) – Director: Herbert L. Strock. Screenplay: Kenneth Langtry.

Ich seh, Ich seh (*Goodnight Mommy*, 2014) – Director: Veronika Franz and Severin Fiala. Screenplay: Veronika Franz and Severin Fiala.

Identity (2003) – Director: James Mangold. Screenplay: Michael Cooney.

Insidious (2010) – Director: James Wan. Screenplay: Leigh Whannell.

Intruder (1989) – Director: Scott Spiegel. Screenplay: Scott Spiegel.

It (2017) – Director: Andy Muschietti. Screenplay: Chase Palmer, Cary Fukunaga and Gary Dauberman.

It Comes at Night (2017) – Director: Trey Edward Shults. Screenplay: Trey Edward Shults.

It Follows (2014) – Director: David Robert Mitchell. Screenplay: David Robert Mitchell.

Jack Frost (1997) – Director: Michael Cooney. Screenplay: Michael Cooney and Jeremy Paige.

Jacob's Ladder (1990) – Director: Adrian Lyne. Screenplay: Bruce Joel Rubin.

Jaws (1975) – Director: Steven Spielberg. Screenplay: Peter Benchley and Carl Gottlieb.

Ju-On: The Grudge (2002) – Director: Takashi Shimizu. Screenplay: Takashi Shimizu.

Junior (1994) – Director: Ivan Reitman. Screenplay: Kevin Wade and Chris Conrad.

Juno (2007) – Director: Jason Reitman. Screenplay: Diablo Cody.

Jurassic Park (1993) – Director: Steven Spielberg. Screenplay: Michael Crichton and David Koepp.

Jurassic World (2015) – Director: Colin Trevorrow. Screenplay: Rick Jaffa, Amanda Silver, Derek Connolly and Colin Trevorrow.

Kairo (*Pulse*, 2001) – Director: Kiyoshi Kurosawa. Screenplay: Kiyoshi Kurosawa.

Killer Klowns from Outer Space (1988) – Director: Stephen Chiodo. Screenplay: Charles Chiodo and Stephen Chiodo.

Killer Workout (*Aerobicide*, 1987) – Director: David A. Prior. Screenplay: David A. Prior.

La Rose de Fer (*The Iron Rose*, 1973) – Director: Jean Rolling. Screenplay: Jean Rollin, Tristan Corbière and Maurice Lemaître.

Leák (*Mystics of Bali*, 1981) – Director: H. Tjut Djalil. Screenplay: Putra Mada and Jimmy Atmaja.

Leprechaun 2 (1994) – Director: Rodman Flender. Screenplay: Turi Meyer and Al Septien.

Long Weekend (1979) – Director: Colin Eggleston. Screenplay: Everett De Roche.

Low Blow (1986) – Director: Frank Harris. Screenplay: Leo Fong.

Madman (1982) – Director: Joe Giannone. Screenplay: Joe Giannone.

C'est Arrivé Près de Chez Vous (*Man Bites Dog*, 1992) – Director: Rémy Belvaux, André Bonzel and Benoît Poelvoorde. Screenplay: Rémy Belvaux, André Bonzel, Benoît Poelvoorde and Vincent Tavier.

Mandy (2018) – Director: Panos Cosmatos. Screenplay: Panos Cosmatos and Aaron Stewart-Ahn.

Maniac (1980) – Director: William Lustif. Screenplay: C. A. Rosenberg and Joe Spinell.

Meek's Cutoff (2010) – Director: Kelly Reichardt. Screenplay: Jonathan Raymond.

Meet the Applegates (1990) – Director: Michael Lehmann. Screenplay: Michael Lehmann and Redbeard Simmons.

Mimic (1997) – Director: Guillermo del Toro. Screenplay: Matthew Robbins and Guillermo del Toro.

Monster (2003) – Director: Patty Jenkins. Screenplay: Patty Jenkins.

Ms. 45 (1981) – Director: Abel Ferrara. Screenplay: Nicholas St. John.

My Bloody Valentine (1981) – Director: George Mihalka. Screenplay: John Beaird.

My Bloody Valentine 3D (2009) – Director: Patrick Lussier. Screenplay: Zane Smith and Todd Farmer.

Natural Born Killers (1994) – Director: Oliver Stone. Screenplay: Richard Rutowski, Oliver Stone and David Veloz.

Night of the Bloody Apes (1969) – Director: René Cardona. Screenplay: René Cardona Jr. and René Cardona.

Night of the Demons (1988) – Director: Kevin S. Tenney. Screenplay: Joe Augustyn.

Night of the Eagle (1962) – Director: Sidney Hayers. Screenplay: Charles Beaumont, Richard Matheson and George Baxt.

Night of the Living Dead (1968) – Director: George A. Romero. Screenplay: George A. Romero and John Russo.

Nightbreed (1990) – Director: Clive Barker. Screenplay: Clive Barker.

Open Water (2003) – Director: Chris Kentis. Screenplay: Chris Kentis.

Orca (1977) – Director: Michael Anderson. Screenplay: Luciano Vincenzoni and Sergio Donati.

Orphan (2009) – Director: Jaume Collet-Serra. Screenplay: David Leslie Johnson.

Ouija (2014) – Director: Stiles White. Screenplay: Juliet Snowden and Stiles White.

Ouija: Origin of Evil (2016) – Director: Mike Flanagan. Screenplay: Mike Flanagan and Jeff Howard.

Paranormal Activity (2007) – Director: Oren Peli. Screenplay: Oren Peli.

Perfect Blue (1998) – Director: Satoshi Kon. Screenplay: Sadayuki Murai.

Pitstop (1969) – Director: Jack Hill. Screenplay: Jack Hill.

Poltergeist (1982) – Director: Tobe Hooper. Screenplay: Steven Spielberg, Michael Grais and Mark Victor.

Poltergeist II: The Other Side (1986) – Director: Brian Gibson. Screenplay: Michael Grais and Mark Victor.

Possession (1981) – Director: Andrzej Żuławski. Screenplay: Frederic Tuten and Andrzej Żuławski.

Prince of Darkness (1987) – Director: John Carpenter. Screenplay: John Carpenter.

Prison (1987) – Director: Renny Harlin. Screenplay: Irwin Yablans and C. Courtney Joyner.

Profondo Rosso (*Deep Red*, 1975) – Director: Dario Argento. Screenplay: Dario Argento and Salvatore Argento.

Prophecy (1979) – Director: John Frankenheimer. Screenplay: David Seltzer.

Psycho (1960) – Director: Alfred Hitchcock. Screenplay: Joseph Stefano.

Pulp Fiction (1994) – Director: Quentin Tarantino. Screenplay: Quentin Tarantino.

Pumpkinhead (1988) – Director: Stan Winston. Screenplay: Stan Winston, Richard C. Weinman, Gary Gerani and Mark Patrick Carducci.

Razorback (1984) – Director: Russell Mulcahy. Screenplay: Everett De Roche.

Red, White & Blue (2010) – Director: Simon Rumley. Screenplay: Simon Rumley.

Repulsion (1965) – Director: Roman Polanski. Screenplay: Roman Polanski, Gérard Brach and David Stone.

Requiem (2006) – Director: Hans-Christian Schmid. Screenplay: Bernd Lange.

Revenge (2017) – Director: Coralie Fargeat. Screenplay: Coralie Fargeat.

Rosemary's Baby (1968) – Director: Roman Polanski.
Screenplay: Roman Polanski.

Satan's Slave (1976) – Director: Norman J. Warren.
Screenplay: David McGillivray.

Saw (2004) – Director: James Wan. Screenplay: Leigh
Whannell.

Scanners (1981) – Director: David Cronenberg.
Screenplay: David Cronenberg.

Schramm (1993) – Director: Jörg Buttgereit.
Screenplay: Jörg Buttgereit and Franz Rodenkirchen.

Scream (1996) – Director: Wes Craven. Screenplay;
Kevin Williamson.

Se7en (1995) – Director: David Fincher. Screenplay:
Andrew Kevin Walker.

Session 9 (2001) – Director: Brad Anderson.
Screenplay: Brad Anderson and Stephen Gevedon.

Shutter (2004) – Director: Banjong Pisanthanakun and
Parkpoom Wongpoom. Screenplay: Banjong
Pisanthanakun, Sopon Sukdapisit and Parkpoom
Wongpoom.

Silence (2016) – Director: Martin Scorsese.
Screenplay: Jay Cocks and Martin Scorsese.

Sleepaway Camp (1983) – Director: Robert Hiltzik.
Screenplay: Robert Hiltzik.

Slugs (1988) – Director: Juan Piquer Simón.
Screenplay: Juan Piquer Simón and Ron Gantman.

Snowtown (2011) – Director: Justin Kurzel.
Screenplay: Shaun Grant.

Somos lo que hay (*We Are What We Are*, 2010) – Director: Jorge Michel Grau. Screenplay: Jorge Michel Grau.

Son of Frankenstein (1939) – Director: Rowland V. Lee. Screenplay: Wyllis Cooper.

Spider (2002) – Director: David Cronenberg. Screenplay: Patrick McGrath.

Spoorloos (*The Vanishing*, 1988) – Director: George Sluizer. Screenplay: George Sluizer and Tim Krabbé.

Squirm (1976) – Director: Jeff Lieberman. Screenplay: Jeff Lieberman.

Star Wars (1977) – Director: George Lucas. Screenplay: George Lucas.

Starry Eyes (2014) – Director: Kevin Kölsch and Dennis Widmyer. Screenplay: Kevin Kölsch and Dennis Widmyer.

Stranger Things (2016-, TV) – Created: The Duffer Brothers

Summer of Sam (1999) – Director: Spike Lee. Screenplay: Victor Colicchio, Michael Imperioli and Spike Lee.

Tarantula! (1955) – Director: Jack Arnold. Screenplay: Robert M. Fresco and Martin Berkeley.

Tenemos la Carne (*We Are the Flesh*, 2016) – Director: Emiliano Rocha Minter. Screenplay: Emiliano Rocha Minter.

Terrore nello Spazio (*Planet of the Vampires*, 1965) – Director: Mario Bava. Screenplay: Ib Melchior, Alberto

Bevilacqua, Callisto Cosulich, Mario Bava, Antonio Roman and Rafael J. Salvia.

The Angry Red Planet (1960) – Director: Ib Melchior. Screenplay: Sidney W. Pink and Ib Melchior.

The Babadook (2014) – Director: Jennifer Kent. Screenplay: Jennifer Kent.

The Blair Witch Project (1999) – Director: Daniel Myrick and Eduardo Sánchez. Screenplay: Daniel Myrick and Eduardo Sánchez.

The Blob (1958) – Director: Irvin Yeaworth. Screenplay: Kay Linaker and Theodore Simonson.

The Burning (1981) – Director: Tony Maylam. Screenplay: Bob Weinstein and Peter Lawrence.

The Bye Bye Man (2017) – Director: Stacy Title. Screenplay: Jonathan Penner.

The Cabin in the Woods (2012) – Director: Drew Goddard. Screenplay: Joss Whedon and Drew Goddard.

The Cell (2000) – Director: Tarsem Singh. Screenplay: Mark Protosevich.

The Changeling (1980) – Director: Peter Medak. Screenplay: Russell Hunter, William Gray and Diana Maddox.

The Collector (2009) – Director: Marcus Dunstan. Screenplay: Marcus Dunstan and Patrick Melton.

The Conjuring (2013) – Director: James Wan. Screenplay: Chad Hayes and Carey W. Hayes.

The Conjuring 2 (2016) – Director: James Wan. Screenplay: Chad Hayes, Carey W. Hayes, James Wan and David Leslie Johnson.

The Craft (1996) – Director: Andrew Fleming. Screenplay: Andrew Fleming and Peter Filardi.

The Crazies (1973) – Director: George A. Romero. Screenplay: Paul McCollough and George A. Romero.

The Curse of Frankenstein (1957) – Director: Terence Fisher. Screenplay: Jimmy Sangster.

The Curse of the Cat People (1944) – Director: Robert Wise and Gunther von Fritsch. Screenplay: DeWitt Bodeen.

The Dark Knight (2008) – Director: Christopher Nolan. Screenplay: Jonathan Nolan and Christopher Nolan.

The Descent (2006) – Director: Neil Marshall. Screenplay: Neil Marshall.

The Devil Rides Out (1968) – Director: Terence Fisher. Screenplay: Richard Matheson.

The Devil's Candy (2015) – Director: Sean Byrne. Screenplay: Sean Byrne.

The Devil's Rain (1975) – Director: Robert Fuest. Screenplay: Gabe Essoe, James Ashton and Gerald Hopman.

The Evil Dead (1981) – Director: Sam Raimi. Screenplay: Sam Raimi.

The Exorcist (1973) – Director: William Friedkin. Screenplay: William Peter Blatty.

The Exorcist III: Legion (1990) – Director: William Peter Blatty. Screenplay: William Peter Blatty.

The Eye (2002) – Director: The Pang Brothers. Screenplay: Jojo Hui and the Pang Brothers.

The Fly (1986) – Director: David Cronenberg. Screenplay: Charles Edward Pogue and David Cronenberg.

The Grudge (2004) – Director: Takashi Shimizu. Screenplay: Stephen Susco.

The Grudge 2 (2006) – Director: Takashi Shimizu. Screenplay: Stephen Susco.

The Guest (2014) – Director: Adam Wingard. Screenplay: Simon Barrett.

The Haunted Castle (1897) – Director: Georges Méliès.

The Haunting (1963) – Director: Robert Wise. Screenplay: Nelson Gidding.

The Hills Have Eyes (1977) – Director: Wes Craven. Screenplay: Wes Craven.

The Hills Have Eyes (2006) – Director: Alexandre Aja. Screenplay: Alexandre Aja and Grégory Levasseur.

The Hillside Strangler (2004) – Director: Chuck Parello. Screenplay: Stephen Johnston.

The Honeymoon Killers (1970) – Director: Leonard Kastle. Screenplay: Leonard Kastle.

The House of the Devil (2009) – Director: Ti West. Screenplay: Ti West.

The Houses that October Built (2014) – Director: Bobby Roe. Screenplay: Zack Andrews, Bobby Roe and Jason Zada.

The Innkeepers (2011) – Director: Ti West. Screenplay: Ti West.

The Innocents (1961) – Director: Jack Clayton. Screenplay: William Archibald, Truman Capote and John Mortimer.

The Last Horror Movie (2003) – Director: Julian Richards. Screenplay: James Handel.

The Last House on the Left (1972) – Director: Wes Craven. Screenplay: Wes Craven.

The Legend of Hell House (1973) – Director: John Hough. Screenplay: Richard Matheson.

The Living Dead at the Manchester Morgue (*Let Sleeping Corpses Lie*, 1974) – Director: Jorge Grau. Screenplay: Juan Cobos, Sandro Continenza, Marcello Coscia and Miguel Rubio.

The Lords of Salem (2012) – Director: Rob Zombie. Screenplay: Rob Zombie.

The Man Who Knew Too Much (1956) – Director: Alfred Hitchcock. Screenplay: John Michael Hayes.

The Mist (2007) – Director: Frank Darabont. Screenplay: Frank Darabont.

The Mummy (2017) – Director: Alex Kurtzman. Screenplay: David Koepp, Christopher McQuarrie and Dylan Kussman.

The Neon Demon (2016) – Director: Nicolas Winding Refn. Screenplay: Mary Laws, Nicholas Winding Refn and Polly Stenham.

The Nest (1988) – Director: Terence H. Winkless. Screenplay: Robert King.

The Nun (2018) – Director: Corin Hardy. Screenplay: Gary Dauberman.

The Omen (1976) – Director: Richard Donner. Screenplay: David Seltzer.

The Omen (2006) – Director: John Moore. Screenplay: David Seltzer.

The Phantom of the Opera (1925) – Director: Rupert Julian. Screenplay: Uncredited.

The Pyramid (2014) –Director: Grégory Levasseur. Screenplay: Daniel Meersand and Nick Simon.

The Return of the Living Dead (1985) – Director: Dan O'Bannon. Screenplay: Dan O'Bannon.

The Ring (2002) – Director: Gore Verbinski. Screenplay: Ehren Kruger.

The Ruins (2008) – Director: Carter Smith. Screenplay: Scott B. Smith.

The Searchers (1956) – Director: John Ford. Screenplay: Frank Nugent.

The Sentinel (1977) – Director: Michael Winner. Screenplay: Jeffrey Konvitz and Michael Winner.

The Shining (1980) – Director: Stanley Kubrick. Screenplay: Stanley Kubrick and Diane Johnson.

The Sixth Sense (1999) – Director: M. Night Shyamalan. Screenplay: M. Night Shyamalan.

The Stand (1994, TV miniseries) – Director: Mick Garris. Screenplay: Stephen King.

The Stepfather (1987) – Director: Joseph Ruben. Screenplay: Donald E. Westlake.

The Stone Tape (1972) – Director: Peter Sasdy. Screenplay: Nigel Kneale.

The Strangers (2008) – Director: Bryan Bertino. Screenplay: Bryan Bertino.

The Terminator (1984) – Director: James Cameron. Screenplay: James Cameron and Gale Anne Hurd.

The Texas Chainsaw Massacre (1974) – Director: Tobe Hooper. Screenplay: Kim Henkel and Tobe Hooper.

The Texas Chainsaw Massacre (2003) – Director: Marcus Nispel. Screenplay: Scott Kosar.

The Thing (1982) – Director: John Carpenter. Screenplay: Bill Lancaster.

The Thing From Another World (1951) – Director: Christian Nyby. Screenplay: Charles Lederer.

The Witch (2015) – Director: Robert Eggers. Screenplay: Robert Eggers.

The Wicker Man (1973) – Director: Robin Hardy. Screenplay: Anthony Shaffer.

Them! (1954) – Director: Gordon Douglas. Screenplay: Ted Sherdeman and Russell Hughes.

Ticks (1993) – Director: Tony Randel. Screenplay: Brent V. Friedman.

To the Devil a Daughter (1976) – Director: Peter Sykes. Screenplay: Chris Wicking, John Peacock and Gerald Vaughan-Huges.

Tremors (1990) – Director: Ron Underwood. Screenplay: Brent Maddock and S. S. Wilson.

The Twilight Zone. "Time Enough at Last" (1959) – Director: John Brahm. Screenplay: Rod Serling.

Videodrome (1983) – Director: David Cronenberg. Screenplay: David Cronenberg.

Warlock (1989) – Director: Steve Miner. Screenplay: David Twohy.

You're Next (2011) – Director: Adam Wingard. Screenplay: Simon Barrett.

Zero Day (2003) – Director: Ben Coccio. Screenplay: Ben Coccio and Christopher Coccio.